About Demos

Demos is a greenhouse for new ideas which can improve the quality of our lives. As an independent think tank, we aim to create an open resource of knowledge and learning that operates beyond traditional party politics.

We connect researchers, thinkers and practitioners to an international network of people changing politics. Our ideas regularly influence government policy, but we also work with companies, NGOs, colleges and professional bodies.

Demos knowledge is organised around five themes, which combine to create new perspectives. The themes are democracy, learning, enterprise, quality of life and global change.

But we also understand that thinking by itself is not enough. Demos has helped to initiate a number of practical projects which are delivering real social benefit through the redesign of public services.

We bring together people from a wide range of backgrounds to cross-fertilise ideas and experience. By working with Demos, our partners develop a sharper insight into the way ideas shape society. For Demos, the process is as important as the final product.

www.demos.co.uk

First published in 2004
© Demos
Some rights reserved – see copyright licence for details

ISBN 1 84180 119 4
Typeset by Land & Unwin, Bugbrooke
Printed by Hendy Banks, London

For further information and
subscription details please contact:

Demos
The Mezzanine
Elizabeth House
39 York Road
London SE1 7NQ

telephone: 020 7401 5330
email: hello@demos.co.uk
web: www.demos.co.uk

Masters of the Universe

Science, politics and the new space race

Melissa Mean and
James Wilsdon

DEMⒸS

Contents

Acknowledgements

This report represents the culmination of a year-long partnership between Demos and the UK space community. We are grateful to all our partners for their support:

EADS Astrium
the British National Space Centre (BNSC)
the Met Office
the Natural Environment Research Council (NERC)
the Particle Physics and Astronomy Research Council (PPARC)
the Rutherford Appleton Laboratory
the Science Museum, London
the UK Industrial Space Committee

Please note that the opinions expressed in this final report are those of the authors and do not necessarily reflect the views of all our partners.

Thanks to those representatives of our partner organisations who sat on the project steering group, and guided the research process from design to completion: Richard Brook (UKISC), Alice Bunn (NERC), Pierre Diederich, Alan Hicks (UKISC), Richard Holdaway (RAL), Sue Johnson (EADS Astrium), Andrew le Masurier (PPARC), Doug Millard (Science Museum, London), Steve Noyes (Met Office), David Parker (EADS Astrium), Jim Sadlier (PPARC) and Martin Shelley (BNSC).

We are particularly grateful to Colin Hicks, Director General of the British National Space Centre, for encouraging us to embark on the project in the first place.

Many other experts participated in the project seminars, or allowed us to interview them, including José Achache, Rachel Armstrong, Ian Becking, Marina Benjamin, Stephen Briggs, Brian Chase, Charles Cockell, Mike Dillon, Jean-Jacques Dordain, Peter Ewins, Kevin Fong, Subrata Ghoshroy, Roy Gibson, Professor Gerry Gilmore, Professor Robert Gurney, Professor Ian Halliday, Professor Ray Harris, Alan Haskell, Anna Hill, Tim Howell, Lord Hunt, Wesley Huntress, Olof Lundberg, Alexsandra Mir, Patrick Moore, Martin O'Neill MP, Pat Norris, Richard Obermann, Franco Ongaro, Colin Paynter, Sir Martin Rees, Lynn Rosentrater, Lord Sainsbury, John Schumacher, Professor David Southwood, Sir Martin Sweeting, John Taylor, Nick Veck, Professor Alan Wells, David Whitehouse, Professor John Zarneki and Robert Zubrin.

At Demos, we thank Tom Bentley, Eddie Gibb, John Holden, Rachel Briggs and Peter MacLeod for their support throughout the project and their helpful comments on earlier drafts. We are grateful to Nicola Wilson and Bobby Webster for assisting with the research and to Andrew Gunn at MORI for coordinating the opinion polling.

Many of those mentioned above will spot where we have drawn from and incorporated their ideas. Any errors or omissions remain entirely our own.

Melissa Mean and James Wilsdon
February 2004

Introduction: four stories of space

There's no point in saying this was a heroic British failure and going back into our shell until 2009. We must push on.

Professor Colin Pillinger, 7 January 2004

Today we set a new course for America's space programme. We will give NASA a new focus and vision for future exploration. We will build new ships to carry man forward into the Universe, to gain a new foothold on the Moon, and to prepare for new journeys to worlds beyond our own.

President George W Bush, 14 January 2004

The year 2003 began and ended with two high-profile failures in space. On 2 February, the space shuttle Columbia disintegrated on its re-entry to Earth's atmosphere, killing all of the astronauts on board. On Christmas Day, many woke expecting to hear Blur's call sign announce the safe arrival of Beagle 2 on the surface of Mars. But the call never came.

These were failures on a very different scale. The first involved the loss of seven lives and unleashed a fierce bout of external criticism and introspection at NASA, the US space agency. The second involved the loss of an unmanned probe no larger than a bicycle wheel. But the response to these failures tells us a lot about the very different place that space exploration occupies in the public consciousness in

America and Britain, and the way it fuels particular notions of national identity.

In the US, eleven months after the Columbia disaster, space was back at the top of the political agenda. The panoramic shots of the Martian landscape taken by NASA's successful Spirit mission provided the perfect backdrop to a high-profile presidential speech. 'Mankind,' declared President Bush, 'is drawn to the heavens for the same reason we were once drawn into unknown lands and across the open sea...So let us continue the journey.'[1] In a staunch defence of the value of space exploration, President Bush announced plans to replace the ageing shuttle with a new generation of spacecraft that by 2020 will enable astronauts to establish a permanent base on the Moon. A series of robotic missions to Mars and beyond will act as stepping stones to the eventual goal: the first astronauts setting foot on Mars by 2030.

Critics have dismissed Bush's speech as a stunt aimed at generating support in an election year, and many questions about the financial and technological viability of his plans remain unanswered. But it still stands as a powerful reminder of the central role that space has played in American politics and culture since the Apollo era. It is impossible to imagine an equivalent speech from Tony Blair.

Bush's sense of ambition also stands in contrast with the British response to Beagle 2. Here, the excitement generated in the run-up to Christmas has quickly faded. In Whitehall there have been mutterings about wasted money and the need to learn lessons for future missions. And Beagle's failure has been made all the more painful by the dual triumph of NASA's Spirit and Opportunity rovers, which are now crawling over the surface of Mars, beaming back stunning images and a rich flow of scientific data.

Yet before we dismiss Beagle as the latest in a line of honourable British failures, it is worth reflecting on some of its more successful aspects. First, Beagle has shown that Britain can play a leadership role in space. Although we invest less in space than most of our European partners – and a tiny fraction of what the Americans spend – Beagle has shown that British scientists can take their place at the forefront of a high-profile European project. It is also important to remember that Beagle was only one element of the larger Mars Express mission, which has significant UK involvement and is so far proving highly successful.

Second, Beagle has dramatically increased public awareness of Britain's involvement in space, and has shown that it is possible to generate similar levels of enthusiasm for robotic missions with a compelling scientific purpose as were generated by human space flight during the Apollo era. This is borne out by a MORI poll of 1,000 adults conducted for Demos in February 2004: 72 per cent of those we surveyed felt that the Beagle mission was interesting and worthwhile, and 66 per cent felt that Britain should try again with new missions.

The Beagle experience has focused attention on some of the long-standing problems of the British space programme, which has skipped a generation by failing to capture the imagination of younger people. This may now be changing, as a new, enthusiastic 'Beagle generation' begins to emerge.

Demos polling shows a distinct generational difference in attitudes to space, with those aged between 16 and 34 more enthusiastic about space than older people, including the 'Apollo generation' of those aged between 35 and 54. People were asked whether Britain should be involved in nine different non-military space activities, ranging from monitoring environmental changes to the Earth and protecting the Earth from asteroids and comets, to building satellites and exploring the Universe with robots and telescopes. Across these nine activities as a whole, 6.7 per cent more people in the 'Beagle generation' felt that Britain should be involved with these activities than those polled aged 35 or over.

By contrast the 'space establishment' is overwhelmingly populated by male scientists approaching retirement age. For years they have been making the argument that space science should be valued for its economic and technological benefits. The unintended effect of this cumulative message was to portray space as 'worthy but dull'.

What the space establishment may have forgotten is that they themselves were raised on stories of Apollo missions to the Moon; non-stick frying pans were a useful spin-off technology rather than the main purpose of the space programme. But this utilitarian view of space has been consistently reinforced by UK government policy, whose approach is best described as 'down to earth'.

With his mutton-chop whiskers and West Country burr, Colin Pillinger is an unlikely ambassador for space. But as the leader of the Beagle team, Pillinger's stroke of genius was to treat space as an extension of show business. Despite his status as an elder statesman of British space science, he recognised something that the space establishment had missed: that reaching out to new audiences was an important component of the programme's long-term success.

In the 1960s, the American space industry became a world-beater, despite losing an early lead to the Soviets, in part because of its ability to enlist the support of the entertainment industry. From Buzz Aldrin to Buzz Lightyear, Hollywood and NASA have enjoyed a mutually reinforcing relationship in portraying a particular version of American heroism in space. Today, NASA is the only public agency in the world with its own cable TV channel.

The champagne may have remained unopened at Beagle HQ, but the mission does appear to have reached out to new audiences and, in doing so, Pillinger has shown that it is possible to build new coalitions of support for space. By enlisting the support of Blur and the artist Damien Hirst, Pillinger displayed a creative flair and an awareness of pop culture that is rare in the dry world of academic science. It was this ability to speak to a new generation that attracted Blur's Alex James to the Beagle project 'Perhaps Colin's greatest achievement is not that he got as far as Mars, but that he got as wide as science, art and music working together,' says James. 'We're all after the same thing, really – life.'[2] The Christmas Day news coverage of Beagle's mission HQ showed scientists mingling with celebrities as they anxiously awaited news of the probe's safe descent. For the first time in years, space seemed fashionable. It was even reported that Kate Moss – the ultimate barometer of style – had received a telescope for Christmas, in order to pursue her new passion for astronomy.

Although he now hangs out with the art school set, Pillinger has cast himself as the quintessential British boffin, the latest in a long line of what Francis Spufford calls the 'Backroom Boys' – 'those quiet men in pullovers…whose imaginings take shape not in words but in mild steel and carbon fibre and lines of code'.[3] By emphasising the initial scepticism he faced from the scientific establishment, Pillinger has played on the stereotype of the plucky inventor. But he has also shown himself to be an accomplished political operator. To get Beagle off the ground, he spent years travelling cap in hand between the research councils, government and industry to persuade them that the project could work. The Cambridge astronomer Paul Murdin observes that 'Colin plays the West country farmer type…but his political knowledge is masterful and he bowled over the Commons select committee when he came to persuade them to back Beagle'.[4]

The money was eventually forthcoming, but Beagle's failure has since raised questions about the sustainability of such a budget model of space exploration. Beagle cost around £45 million, less than a tenth of what NASA spent on its Spirit and Opportunity rovers. The challenge now confronting British space policy is to make it easier next time around. Rather than going down in history as a valiant failure, Beagle should mark the beginning of a new chapter for Britain in space. For too long we have been reluctant bystanders, failing to accord space the economic and political priority it deserves. Despite New Labour's general support for science, space has not risen in profile over the past six years, and has formed no part of the government's wider political or technological narrative. The UK languishes near the bottom of the league table of investment in space, spending less as a proportion of GDP than France, Germany or Italy. Even India and Belgium spend more.[5]

After Beagle: what next for Britain in space?

The strength of the public response to Beagle should be a wake-up call to policy-makers. Space is an important yet neglected part of the public realm. As the last unexplored commons, it exerts a powerful hold on our social imagination. And the study of the solar system poses fundamental questions, not only for science, but also for philosophical and religious accounts of the origins and significance of human life.

Since the sixteenth century, when Copernicus first argued that the Earth circles the Sun rather than vice versa, our understanding of ourselves as central to the Universe has gradually eroded. First came the understanding that every star is a sun just like our own; then that we are part of just one galaxy among many. Over the past decade scientists have come to accept that even the matter we are made of is not the majority experience of the Universe. And within the next few years many scientists believe that we will discover evidence of life beyond Earth. Sir Martin Rees, the Astronomer Royal, argues that this 'quest for alien life is, in my view, entirely justified – indeed it is surely among the most fascinating challenges to science in the twenty-first century'.[6]

Robotic missions may lack some of the glamour of human exploration, but they are easily the most practical and cost-effective way of deepening our understanding of the solar system. Beagle 2 marked the start of an intensive burst of activity, which will include a series of ground-breaking robotic missions over the next two years. In recent months, NASA's Spirit and Opportunity missions to Mars have been followed by the Stardust probe and the launch of the Rosetta comet-chaser. In July 2004 the Cassini-Huygens spacecraft – a joint project of NASA and the European Space Agency (ESA) – arrives at Saturn, and will deliver the Huygens probe into the atmosphere of Titan, one of Saturn's moons. Then in 2005 ESA's Smart 1 craft will head for the Moon and the Venus Express probe will be launched.

British scientists are involved in each of these missions. All of them are risky and some will almost inevitably fail. When confronted with a difficult task, we sometimes say 'It isn't rocket science', but this *is* rocket science: each of these missions relies on highly complex instruments capable of operating in hostile environments millions of miles from Earth. As part of a renewed commitment to space, the UK needs to develop a more entrepreneurial, risk-taking approach. There is much to learn from the American ability to bounce back from disaster. In 1999 NASA lost four Mars missions in less than three months at a cost of $300 million. Four years later it was able to celebrate the success of Spirit and Opportunity.

Despite the loss of Beagle, Britain needs to start investing now to ensure success five or ten years down the line. Colin Pillinger has already said that he would prefer not to wait for ESA's next mission to Mars in 2009, but would like to launch a new probe by 2007 using the same innovative technology. Although it was comparatively cheap, Beagle was more sophisticated than anything NASA has deployed, and would have been capable of digging beneath the surface of Mars to sniff for chemical signs of life. Our MORI poll indicates there is strong public support for a Beagle 3 mission, with 66 per cent of respondents feeling that it is important for Britain to try again.

But before it starts investing in new missions Britain needs a distinctive account of why space matters. This can only be developed by first understanding what others are saying. Below we outline three influential narratives about space – the 'final frontier', 'down to earth' and 'space wars' – and then sketch out a progressive vision of 'public space', which Britain can make its own.

The final frontier

On 12 September 1962, in an emotive speech at Rice University in Texas, President Kennedy outlined his ambitions for the US space programme. Speaking at the height of the Cold War, he urged the two great superpowers to direct their rivalries upwards rather than outwards – towards the uncharted expanses of the solar system. He insisted that America would claim its position as 'the world's leading spacefaring nation', but softened this flag-waving with a more conciliatory message that: 'space can be explored and mastered without feeding the fires of war, without repeating the mistakes that man has made in extending his writ around this globe of ours.'[7]

At the time, the Soviets were winning the space race hands down. The first Sputnik satellite entered orbit in 1957, and four years later the cosmonaut Yuri Gagarin became the first man in space. JF

Kennedy responded with the bold pledge that the US would send a man to the Moon 'before this decade is out'; a promise that was eventually fulfilled on 20 July 1969, when Apollo 11 commander Neil Armstrong took a few dusty steps on the Moon.

An entire generation was spellbound by the grainy TV footage of the Apollo missions. It seemed as if a new chapter in human history was beginning, which would see humans travel first to the Moon, then to Mars, and eventually to the outer reaches of the solar system.

What few could have realised was that the Apollo programme represented not the beginning but the end of a particular story of space – what we might call the *final frontier* – which saw space exploration as the next step in a journey of discovery that had propelled us from caves into skyscrapers. It was a particularly American story – that tapped into powerful currents of national myth about the frontier spirit of the Pilgrim Fathers and the cowboys. But for a time it captured the imagination of the world.

However, JFK's 1962 speech was the highwater mark of a tide of political enthusiasm for space, which was soon to ebb away. Before Neil Armstrong had even taken his 'giant leap for mankind', Richard Nixon was already scaling back US funding for space in order to deal with recession at home and an escalating war in Vietnam.

Over the next four decades the frontier vision gradually faded. No one under age 35 can now remember when men walked on the Moon. Human space flight continues, but has lost any overall sense of purpose, failing to excite much public interest except when disaster strikes. And NASA is widely felt to have lost its way. In recent years it has gone chronically over budget and has failed to outline a clear strategy for US activities in space. Many of its financial woes can be attributed to the cost overruns of the International Space Station but, as the recent report into the Columbia disaster argued, there are also deeper management problems within the organisation.

Marina Benjamin sums up the sense of anti-climax that many of her generation feel: 'Recovering space fanatics like me...grew up dreaming of the cosmic conquest NASA laid out before us in the 60s –

today the Moon, tomorrow lunar bases, space stations and inter-galactic joy rides…By now, we believed we would be seeing routine missions to Mars and projects to colonise more distant worlds. Instead, we never got past first base.'[8]

Until recently the remaining torchbearers of the final frontier were the space lobby groups, which have done their best to keep the keep the dream of JFK's 1962 speech alive. A good example is the Space Frontier Association, which is founded on a set of five propositions:

- ○ It is human destiny to open the space frontier.
- ○ This must be achieved within 50 to 100 years.
- ○ America, as a frontier nation, has a special responsibility to open this frontier.
- ○ The current US space programme is not doing so.
- ○ It must be replaced with one that will.[9]

Another torchbearer is the National Space Society, whose director, Brian Chase, explained to us that: 'Space exploration is the hallmark of a civilized nation. It is part of what it means to be a nation. To innovate, to experiment, to explore new frontiers.' But even he accepts that there is a long way to go: 'If the colonization of space is step 100, we're on about step 12 or 13 right now.'[10]

The last attempt to reignite the frontier vision was made by the first President Bush in 1989. On the 20th anniversary of the Moon landings he set out the goal of completing the Space Station in the 1990s, establishing a permanent presence on the Moon, and then directing efforts to the human exploration of Mars. But this ambition was backed up with little political pressure and even less hard cash. When NASA came back with an estimated bill of $450 billion, the plan was quietly shelved.

Fifteen years later his son has attempted a similar manoeuvre. George W Bush's speech of 14 January 2004 represents the boldest reaffirmation of the frontier vision since the 1960s. Indeed, many commentators felt Bush was making a deliberate attempt to conjure up the spirit of JFK. Taken at face value, his speech offers a clear set of priorities for NASA over the next two decades: to complete the International Space Station by 2010; to develop a new manned exploration vehicle that can replace the space shuttle; to return to the Moon by 2015 and eventually establish a permanent moon base; and, finally, to get astronauts to Mars. Whether any of it actually happens depends on the President's willingness to push it through a sceptical Congress. Contrary to the predictions of Republican strategists, the speech received a decidedly lukewarm reception from the American public, so the smart money says that the son's proposals will go the way of the father's.

Yet the frontier vision is not only enjoying a renaissance in the White House. It is also high on the political agenda in Beijing. On 16 October 2003 Yang Liwei became the first Chinese astronaut in space, spending a total of 21 hours in orbit. The success of his mission sparked a frenzy of speculation about China's longer-term ambitions in space. Ouyang Ziyuan, head of China's moon exploration pro-gramme, has stated that China wants to send a man to the Moon by 2010. A robotic moon probe is predicted by 2008, ideally to coincide with the Beijing Olympics. China appears to understand very well the prestige that can flow from exercising power in space. For now, the frontier vision is alive and kicking.

Down to earth

Despite the ambitions of the US and Chinese governments, the broad thrust of space policy in recent decades has been away from grandiose schemes and lofty speeches towards a utilitarian focus on the technologies and services that space can provide. According to the 'down to earth' narrative, space is of little value in and of itself, unless it can provide spin-off benefits for the economy or society. Today, this is the dominant view of space agencies and companies across the world. It brings with it a policy and institutional orientation that seeks to maximise the contribution space can make to tele-communications, navigation and environmental monitoring.

The precise blend of frontier spirit and utilitarian pragmatism varies from country to country. The Americans and French retain elements of the former within a predominantly utilitarian framework, and there is also a whiff of frontierism in the policies of emerging space nations such as China and India.

But by far the staunchest proponents of the down to earth view are the British. The first paragraph of the UK's draft space strategy makes this position very clear: 'The UK has taken a distinctive approach to space. We have identified clear scientific and commercial objectives for which space activities are the most effective tool, rather than considering space exploration as an end in itself. The uses and users of space have consistently been at the forefront of UK policy.'[11] Similarly, Lord Sainsbury, the UK's Science Minister, has spoken repeatedly about the importance of using space 'as a tool – for scientific, commercial and environmental purposes'.[12]

Although now articulated with greater clarity, this has long been the UK's position. Indeed, it is fair to say that the British have never had a national passion for space, but have always preferred a collaborative approach, either through links to NASA or through the ESA, of which Britain was a founder member. Within ESA the UK has been highly selective in the activities it has chosen to support and has refused to fund several key missions, such as Hermes and Ariane 5. In 1987 Kenneth Clarke, despite his pro-European credentials, decried ESA as 'a hugely expensive club' in which he was 'happy for Britain to remain a passenger'.

For a brief period in the mid-1980s it looked for a brief time as if British policy would change. The British National Space Centre (BNSC) was created in 1985 as an umbrella body for government departments and other key partners with an active stake in space. Under the leadership of Roy Gibson, its first director-general, the BNSC produced a 15-year space plan, which is believed to have called for a trebling of Britain's space budget from £100 million to £300 million a year, a hike in the UK's contribution to ESA to a level commensurate with other European countries, a commitment to independent UK launch capabilities and support for the International Space Station.

Perhaps unsurprisingly, the plan was ill-received by Mrs Thatcher's

Cabinet, and never saw the light of day. The down to earth view continues to hold sway, and Britain goes on providing targeted support for those aspects of space that it deems scientifically or commercially significant.

Little has changed under New Labour. Despite the Blair government's enthusiastic advocacy of new technologies, particularly biotechnology and information technology, space has not risen in political profile over the past six years. As Science Minister, Lord Sainsbury has been a positive force, bringing greater coherence to space policy, but there have been no white papers, no prime ministerial speeches, no Space Envoys. As Martin O'Neill MP observes, 'The modesty of the UK's ambition in space is reflected in the amount of time politicians devote to it.'[13] In July 2000 the Trade and Industry Select Committee produced its first report on space since 1988, but this was not debated by Parliament until the following February.

If you ask a young MP or policy adviser about the future of Britain's space programme, the chances are you will be met with a blank look, or at best an embarrassed smile. Space is too redolent of Harold Wilson's 'white heat of technology' to merit any serious discussion in Blair's Britain. Today, the assumption is that nano-technology and 3G phones hold far greater promise than rocket launchers and satellite systems.

Yet the reality is that space has never been more important to the economic and social well-being of the UK. From the ubiquity of satellite television and the growing availability of broadband in rural areas, to the improved accuracy of weather forecasts and the introduction of GPS-based taxi services, space is already woven into the fabric and texture of our national life and is set to become even more significant over the next 10 to 15 years.

Why is there such a poor understanding of space? In part, because of the space community's failure to communicate its significance. As one government adviser told us, 'The space community is appallingly bad at plugging into wider currents of politics and public policy... They are incredibly insular, they seem to want to stay in their own world. Most people within government don't understand what space is for, what BNSC does, what the money is spent on, or how it contributes to government's wider agenda.'[14]

There is a paradox in the down to earth view. Although it is sensible to highlight the concrete benefits of space, an exclusive focus on these at the expense of the inspirational aspects of space actually serves to undermine the longer-term political and public support on which the practical case rests. To put it another way, if unlocking the full economic and social potential of space relies on higher levels of public support, it is not possible to rely solely on practical examples in order to win people around. The 'vision thing' remains key, and it is this that is lacking from the UK's current approach. Space is not perceived as part of the public domain or as a legitimate subject of political and social aspirations.

Officially, the UK does have a vision for space. It runs as follows: 'The UK will be the most developed user of space-based systems in Europe for science, enterprise and environment. UK citizens will provide and exploit the advanced space-based systems and services which will stimulate innovation in the knowledge-driven society.'[15] None of this is wrong; it all makes perfect sense. But the danger is of it being so sensible that it fails to ignite any new public or political enthusiasm for space.

Space wars

Far away from the practical world of the BNSC, a darker story about space is being written. Within the current US administration, space wars are viewed as an increasingly realistic proposition. This story about space is linked in part to the repercussions of the terrorist attacks of 11 September 2001. But its roots can be traced to before President Bush took office.

In the dying days of the Clinton administration, a neo-conservative think tank called The Project for the New American Century published the report *Rebuilding America's Defences.*[16] Heavily influenced by Dick Cheney, Donald Rumsfeld and Paul Wolfowitz, this report has become notorious for its explicit argument in favour of a second Gulf War. But the penultimate chapter of the report has attracted less attention. Here, the authors argue for a massive scaling up of missile defence systems. These would operate at various levels: lower-tier, ground-based interceptors; upper-tier, plane-based defences, which could target ballistic missiles; and space-based satellite systems, capable of intercepting and destroying enemy missiles immediately after launch.

The report states that: 'No system of missile defences can be fully effective without placing sensors and weapons in space...For US armed forces to continue to assert military pre-eminence, control of space...must be an essential element of our military strategy.'[17] It acknowledges that this will inevitably require the use of force within space and from space, and calls for the creation of a new US space force as a separate service alongside the army, navy and air force. It also questions whether NASA should remain independent of these wider military and strategic priorities.

Immediately before taking office Donald Rumsfeld chaired a high-level space commission, whose final report gives further insights into the current administration's thinking. The commission ominously predicts, 'every medium – air, land and sea – has seen conflict. Reality indicates that space will be no different. Given this virtual certainty, the US must develop the means both to deter and to defend against hostile acts in and from space.' In order to avoid what it terms a 'Space Pearl Harbor', the report calls for the US to develop superior capabilities, able to 'negate the hostile use of space against US interests'.[18]

Against the backdrop of the biggest increase in US defence spending for over 20 years – reaching a total of $399 billion in 2004[19] – there is also a discernible shift in relations between the US Department of Defense and NASA. Although in theory their missions remain quite distinct, a recent ESA survey notes diplomatically that 'new modes of cooperation between America's civilian and military space programmes are currently being explored'[20] and, in November 2002, a new agreement was signed between the two organisations to formalise their closer working arrangements.

It is important in this context to distinguish between *militarisation* and *weaponisation*. Space is already militarised – and has been for decades – in the sense that many satellite systems are used for security and defence purposes. Some are designed exclusively for military use, but many others are 'dual-use', serving both military and civilian purposes. But weaponisation goes a lot further than this. It can be defined as the testing or deployment of technologies specifically designed to fight a war in or from space, or military capabilities on the ground specifically designed to attack satellites in space. A recent report from the Stimson Center suggests that space weaponisation 'exists along a continuum, with the power projection capabilities deemed necessary by the Rumsfeld Commission constituting one end of this spectrum'.[21]

Until now we have not travelled far along that continuum. But this could change rapidly if the hawks in the US administration get their way. Several commentators have interpreted the US withdrawal from the Anti-Ballistic Missiles (ABM) Treaty in December 2001 as a first step towards the development and testing of a new generation of space weapons. Having jettisoned the limited concept of 'national missile defence' advocated by the Clinton administration, President Bush has instead proposed a multi-tiered missile defence system to use 'all available technologies and basing modes for effective missile defences'.[22]

The initial layer of this missile architecture is already in place at Fort Greely in Alaska and Vandenberg Airforce Base in California, where interceptors now exist to target mid-flight ballistic missiles. In parallel with this ground-based system, however, the US is also pushing for a space-based intercept capability that would require weapons to be placed in space. Paul Wolfowitz, Rumsfeld's deputy, has confirmed the administration's desire to see weapons in space as part of a multi-layered missile defence system. 'As we look ahead, we need to think about areas that would provide higher leverage. Nowhere is that more true than in space...It truly is the ultimate high ground. We are exploring concepts and technologies for space-based intercepts.'[23]

Yet any moves in this direction would flout the Outer Space Treaty of 1967, which requires space activities to have 'peaceful purposes'.[24] Weaponisation is also opposed by almost every other nation. A UN resolution on the subject was passed in November 2000 with the support of 163 nations. Only the US and Israel abstained.[25] In Europe, President Chirac has warned that weaponisation 'cannot fail to relaunch the arms race in the world'.[26]

MORI polling for Demos has uncovered a genuine concern among the British public about the militarisation of space: 66 per cent feel that space should be a neutral place, with no military uses, and 68 per cent are concerned that the US is 'more interested in the military potential of space than in sending astronauts to Mars'.

But if the US moves decisively in this direction, space wars may yet come to be the dominant vision of space in the twenty-first century, obscuring its broader economic and social potential. There is no doubt that Europe and China are also weighing up the military potential of space. Speaking in October 2002 at a conference to mark the 35th anniversary of the Outer Space Treaty, Jayantha Dhanapala, the UN's Under-Secretary-General for Disarmament Affairs warned: 'Deployment of weapons in space by one country will spur others to follow. The resulting arms race would lead to incalculable consequences for development and human security and could very well deprive humanity of all the benefits of the peaceful use and exploration of space.'[27]

The 1967 Outer Space Treaty

This provides the basic framework of international space law, including the following principles:

The exploration and use of outer space shall be carried out for the benefit and in the interests of all countries and shall be the province of all mankind.
Outer space shall be free for exploration and use by all states.
Outer space is not subject to national appropriation by claim of

sovereignty, by means of use of occupation, or by any other means. States shall not place nuclear weapons or other weapons of mass destruction in orbit or on celestial bodies or station them in outer space in any other manner.

The Moon and other celestial bodies shall be used exclusively for peaceful purposes.

Astronauts shall be regarded as the envoys of mankind.

Public space

This report argues that the time is now right for a new story about public space. We reject the gung-ho optimism of the final frontier, but also the narrow pragmatism of remaining down to earth. And we stand opposed to space wars and to any escalation in the weaponisation of space. Instead, we want to reconnect space to broader currents of progressive politics. Our account of public space draws on the inspiration of the frontier spirit, but harnesses this in pursuit of practical goals. It consists of the following five dimensions.

1. *It is distinctively European, grounded in the values of peace, prosperity and freedom, with a strong commitment to international development and environmental protection*
    Despite the dominance of the US within the space sector, Europe can provide a different path for the development of space in the service of citizens. This will require revisiting European space budgets and scaling them up to meet new ambitions.

2. *It views space as crucial to the architecture of the smart state*
    The space industry is an important contributor to GDP, a source of innovation, and a provider of high-value, knowledge-based jobs. Space technologies and services will play an increasingly important role in the modernisation of our economy and public services – for example, through satellite-based congestion charging.

They are also vital for sustainable development, enabling us to monitor and manage the health of our ecosystems.

3. *It recognises the intrinsic importance of space science and earth observation, which can help us to understand the origins of the Universe, our place within it and the biophysical systems which underpin life on Earth*
    With exciting breakthroughs anticipated over the next decade, it should be possible to generate a sense of awe and inspiration around space science and earth observation in the way that the early Apollo missions achieved this in the 1960s.

4. *It draws upon the social and cultural power of space, as one way of building public support*
    While investment in space has ebbed and flowed over the past 40 years, our appetite for space in films, TV programmes, books and games has remained constant. The space community has too often dismissed the cultural aspects of space as trivial and unimportant, rather than embracing them as a potent source of innovation and inspiration. The challenge for the future is to reclaim space as part of the public realm.

5. *It democratises space, reclaiming it as part of a progressive political agenda, and developing new forms of participation that allow ordinary citizens to shape the future direction of space research and technology*
    Much can be learned from other areas of science, where processes of public dialogue have become hugely important in recent years. The space community could also learn from the open source model of software development in dissolving expert–citizen divides, and inviting greater public involvement in space research.

Each of these five dimensions is explored in detail in the chapters that follow. The final chapter recommends a series of practical steps that government and the space community could take to realise our vision of public space.

Project methodology

During our research, Demos interviewed more than 70 experts from government, industry and academia. Some of these are on the record, others are unattributed.

In the spring and early summer of 2003, we ran a series of three seminars on the economic, social and environmental dimensions of space, which were attended by 150 people, drawn from within and beyond the UK space community.

We also undertook a series of fact-finding missions to explore the international dimensions of space policy: to ESA in Paris; to Washington DC, where we met NASA officials and a range of US-based space organisations; and to Brussels to meet representatives of the European Commission and developers of new space application.

In the closing stages of the project we commissioned MORI to analyse public perceptions of space. MORI's survey was carried out between 6 and 10 February 2004 on a nationally representative sample of 1,000 adults aged 16 or over.

1. The Eurovision space contest: navigating the geopolitics of space

Jean-Jacques Dordain is a man with a plan. Sitting in his Paris office on a bright June morning, he reflects on the task that awaits him. In four days' time, he takes over as director-general of the European Space Agency. Sitting at the top of his in-tray will be the European space strategy, which was published in draft in early 2003 and is now the focus of debate across Europe's space community.[28]

The draft strategy raises many questions. How ambitious does Europe want to be in space? What is the right balance between European autonomy and cooperation with the US? Can Europe maintain its own launcher capacity? Should it reduce its commitment to human space flight?

Dordain knows that he has to come up with some answers. And he knows that he is taking over at a time of institutional upheaval, as ESA jostles with the European Commission for overall control of European space policy. Yet, despite these challenges, Dordain has a clear picture of what he wants to achieve: a European space programme based around economic innovation, social progress and environmental sustainability.

He rejects the idea that Europe will be forced to follow the path laid down by the US:

> *Europe shouldn't be trying to catch up with the US. For the US, space is an instrument of domination – information domination*

and leadership. But space enables the opposite kind of leadership…it is the best way to distribute information, closing the gap between the information-rich North and the information-poor South…Europe should be proposing a different model: space as a public good.[29]

If you glance through the glossy brochures produced by ESA and NASA you could be forgiven for thinking that Europe and the US have identical approaches to space. They both feature the same shots of gleaming satellites, astronauts talking to children and images of distant planets. They both repeat the mantra of exploration, education, inspiration, industry and collaboration. But probe a little deeper and the differences become sharper. In space, to borrow an argument from the US commentator Robert Kagan, *America is from Mars and Europe is from Venus.*

Kagan's book *Paradise and Power* sparked controversy on both sides of the Atlantic. It opens with a bold assertion:

It is time to stop pretending that Europeans and Americans share a common view of the world, or even that they occupy the same world. On the all-important question of power – the efficacy of power, the morality of power, the desirability of power – American and European perspectives are diverging…That is why on major strategic and international questions today, Americans are from Mars and Europeans are from Venus: they agree on little and understand one another less and less.[30]

Kagan argues that the US divides the world into friends and enemies, prefers unilateralist solutions, favours policies of coercion over diplomacy, and resorts to force more quickly. Europe, on the other hand, has a more complex picture of the world, prefers multilateral solutions, favours negotiation and diplomacy over coercion, and tends to emphasise processes over results.

He acknowledges that his argument contains 'its share of exaggerations and oversimplifications'. Britain, for example, may have a more 'American' view of power than France or Germany. Yet 'the caricatures do capture an essential truth: the US and Europe are fundamentally different today'.[31] And these differences appear to be growing.

Within space policy, you do not have to look far to find evidence of transatlantic tension. The European space strategy argues that the US 'uses space systems as an instrument for guaranteeing strategic, political, scientific and economic leadership combining the concepts of "space dominance" with "information dominance"'.[32] It acknowledges that Europe has enjoyed the 'privileged' status of a close ally, but goes on to suggest that:

> 'These relations have nevertheless been marked by a constant desire on the part of the Americans to be pre-eminent in space… NASA expects to remain in control of design, development and means of launch, such that Europe contributes to the less strategic aspects of space missions.'[33]

Such a frank admission in the pages of a European Commission green paper highlights the extent to which US and European ambitions for space have diverged.

Mars: the quest for dominance

This widening gulf became apparent in December 2001 when a letter from Paul Wolfowitz, the US Deputy Secretary of Defence, landed on the desks of Europe's 15 defence ministers. The letter spelt out in blunt terms Washington's opposition to Europe's proposal for a new satellite navigation system.

Known as Galileo, this new system is Europe's passport to an independent future in space. Its constellation of 30 satellites orbiting at an altitude of 24,000 km will broadcast positioning signals across the entire surface of the Earth. This will revolutionise the reach and accuracy of location-based services, from in-car navigation to the tracking of hazardous waste. It is also expected to create 100,000 new jobs.

Washington doesn't like Galileo because it will end the monopoly of its global positioning system (GPS). Conceived in the late 1970s by the US Department of Defense, this system has two service levels, a restricted one for the military and an open one, which is free for civilian use. Currently, the US government can pick and choose which nations use the military channel and it can jam the civilian channel wherever and whenever it wants to. US industry also produces and maintains all the space and ground-control infrastructure that GPS relies on.

Wolfowitz's letter prompted a sharp response, particularly from the French government. President Chirac insisted that the failure of Galileo would reduce Europe 'to a vassal status, first scientific and technical and then industrial and economic'.[34] But the spat over Galileo is about more than just the usual jockeying for power between Europe and the US. It also presents a fundamental choice between open and closed models of innovation. The GPS was designed as a closed, military system and has only ever provided civilian users with a simplified version of its available capabilities. The US has never hesitated to use the GPS to support its strategic interests, and has always retained the option to turn the system off in particular regions at times of conflict or terrorist attack.

When Galileo goes live in 2008, Europe will not only have a superior system in technological terms, but the US will no longer have a finger on the on–off switch. David Braunschvig, a senior member of the US Council of Foreign Relations, acknowledges the threat to US supremacy: 'The Galileo challenge raises the question as to whether the US will continue to enjoy its current dominance in providing the global standard for positioning, timing and navigation. That is why the Pentagon is so nervous.'[35] It is also why, as René Oosterlick, Head of Navigation at ESA, put it when we spoke to him 'the US has done everything it can to kill the project'.[36]

And Galileo is by no means the only example of US efforts to promote a closed model of innovation in space. During the Afghanistan war in 2001 the Pentagon signed an exclusive deal with Space Imaging, a US company that sells photographs from its Ikonos satellite. At a resolution of one metre, these were the best available pictures on the commercial market. For the duration of the war, at a cost of over $2 million a month, the Pentagon paid Space Imaging for control of all high-quality images of Afghanistan.

While there were legitimate security interests at stake, this blanket control also meant that humanitarian groups were denied access to information that could have helped them locate the large number of refugees created by the war. It also prevented the media from verifying the results of American bombing, in particular claims and counter-claims about the number of civilian casualties. One commentator likened the agreement with Space Imaging to 'the government simply buying up all the printing presses in order to prevent critical stories from being printed'.[37]

The European space strategy identifies the underlying reason for such actions. It is the US desire for dominance and control. As Robert Kagan writes: 'Americans seek to defend and advance a liberal international order. But the only stable and successful international order Americans can imagine is one that has the United States at its centre. Nor can Americans conceive of an international order that is not defended by power, and specifically by American power.'[38] US power is now so dominant that any threats it faces are inevitably asymmetric in nature. As a result, the US neither seeks nor expects a level playing field – on Earth or in space.[39]

Nowhere is this strategy of dominance more apparent than in the drive to weaponise space. As security analyst Rebecca Johnson argues, the ambitions of the US administration in this regard are based on three assumptions:

○　*control* – that controlling space will secure unrivalled military and commercial advantages on Earth
○　*vulnerability* – that reliance on space assets presents particular weaknesses, such as attacks on satellite networks
○　*inevitability* – that space weapons are a natural development from land, sea and air weapons.[40]

Yet these assumptions are open to challenge. In a report from the Washington-based Stimson Center, Michael Krepon and Christopher Clary question the inevitability of weaponisation. 'If terrestrial military superiority can continue to be extended without taking the lead in weaponising space, is the latter warranted? And might it be possible that US terrestrial military dominance could be greatly and unnecessarily complicated by weaponising space? Put another way, how much dominance is enough?'[41] Krepon and Clary argue that weaponisation could undermine scientific and commercial uses of space, by heightening insecurity and international tension. In place of a US policy based on space dominance, they call for one based on space assurance:

> Space assurance, unlike space dominance, holds the promise that the weaponisation of space can be avoided...Space assurance, unlike space dominance, provides an environment better suited for commercial gain and scientific discovery...In contrast, efforts to dominate space will likely elevate into the heavens the hair-trigger environment that plagued the superpowers during the Cold War.[42]

It remains to be seen whether such proposals can get a serious hearing in the White House. For now, in line with Donald Rumsfeld's fears of a 'space Pearl Harbor', dominance remains the default operating mode. A key question is whether Europe can offer a viable, alternative path.

Venus: placing space at the service of citizens

In space, as in many areas of policy, Europe is instinctively more open. The preamble to the draft European Constitution states that it 'wishes to remain a continent open to culture, learning and social progress; and...wishes to deepen the democratic and transparent nature of its public life, and to strive for peace, justice and solidarity throughout the world'.[43] The European Union represents a commitment to a set of distinctive values: democracy, coexistence and cooperation between nations that have learned from a history of conflict.[44]

Interpretations of these values vary. Nick Butler detects in the EU 'the pragmatic tone of a continent that understands power all too well and that is sceptical of all who claim to have mastered its use'.[45] But for Robert Kagan, the fact that 'Europeans today are not ambitious for power' is a sign of weakness. As is Europe's failure to recognise the extent to which its values, which it likes to feel are markedly different from those of the US, are in fact entirely reliant on US hegemony: 'American power made it possible for Europeans to believe that power was no longer important.'[46]

So is there – as Kagan would suggest – no alternative for Europe other than facing up to the realities of US dominance? Talking to the top brass at the European Space Agency you get a clear sense that they do believe in an alternative path, that with the right combination of political will and investment, Jean-Jacques Dordain's vision of space as a 'public good' can be achieved.

Galileo is a case in point. As well as being a technologically superior system, it represents a statement of how Europe wants to do things differently. Galileo will be a civilian-controlled system, designed with civilian users in mind. It is the product of collaboration between scientists and industrialists from across the EU. The collaborative sphere has been extended still further by China's recent decision to invest €230 million in the project. Similar discussions are ongoing with India and Israel. All these countries are excluded from participating in the development of the GPS because it is so closely allied to US defence interests.

Galileo represents a shining example of what Henry Chesbrough at the Harvard Business School calls 'open innovation'. Chesbrough argues that we are witnessing a paradigm shift in the way that innovations occur. The old paradigm – of closed innovation – was based on the view that successful innovation requires control. It assumed that firms – or we might add in the context of space policy, nations – must be self-reliant 'because one cannot be sure of the quality, availability and capability of others' ideas: "If you want something done right, you've got to do it yourself.'"[47] Open innovation, on the other hand, assumes that firms – or nations – should combine external and internal ideas into new architectures and systems.

This orientation towards openness and collaboration can be traced back to the origins of the European Space Agency. ESA was born in 1975, at a time when space was still an important arena for Cold War rivalries. Within the US and the Soviet Union achievements in civilian space, including moon exploration, earth observation and telecommunications, were largely spin-offs from the military programme. By contrast, ESA's convention commits it to a strictly civilian mission, with each of its 15 members promising to promote cooperation in space for peaceful purposes. Interdependence is built into its very architecture.

These civilian roots have shaped the aspirations of Europe's space programme for the past 25 years. In the EU space strategy three goals stand out: a collaborative approach to scientific excellence; a desire to place space at the service of citizens; and an emphasis on sustainable development. Antonio Rodotà, the former director-general of ESA, summed up this collaborative spirit: 'Travel to any of ESA's centres and you'll find teams of experts from various nations working successfully together. Please don't forget how amazing that is. Their grandparents were shooting at one another.'[48]

One project that meets all three of these goals is ESA's Global Monitoring for Environment and Security programme (GMES). Currently under development, GMES will be fully operational by 2008. It will integrate space-based and ground-based observation technologies to create a new decision-making tool for use at a European-wide level and beyond. Its priorities include helping to manage natural and man-made disasters (such as floods, earthquakes, fires, oil spills and volcanoes), and monitoring environmental systems including the oceans and atmosphere.

GMES will represent a significant advance on ESA-backed systems such as UNOSAT, which already provide satellite-derived data to aid agencies working on the ground. If there is a disaster such services can mean the difference between life and death. For example, when Hurricane Mitch tore through Central America in November 1998, killing around 10,000 people, UNOSAT was able to provide high-quality images of the region within hours, to help agencies get relief directly to the victims.[49]

The use of space technologies to tackle such problems lies at the heart of the European approach to space, and stands in contrast with a US vision which would see space increasingly dominated by military priorities and closed systems of innovation. The question is: will Mars or Venus win out? Whose story will end up shaping our approach to space in the twenty-first century?

A lot will hinge on the momentum that can be generated by the new EU space strategy, which was published in its final form in November 2003. It remains to be seen whether this will galvanise fresh political and public support for space. For example, moving GMES from strategy documents to operations and implementation is proving slow. While there is an influential body of opinion that recognises fundamental synergies between space and the wider European project – as reflected in the two references to space which Valery Giscard d'Estaing included in an early draft of the EU Constitution[50] – it is important not to underestimate the scale of the challenge. As the EU space strategy argues:

> the fundamental question is that of European ambition. No European nation is capable of independently maintaining a space policy at the necessary level. That the US devotes six times as much in terms of public resources to space as all European countries put together means that Europe cannot remain indifferent if it wishes to play a role.[51]

Piggy in the middle?
Britain could play a decisive role in tipping the balance towards Mars or Venus. However, on questions of space, as with euro entry or the Iraq war, Britain suffers from an identity crisis. Unsure if it wants to be Martian or Venutian, it hovers somewhere between the two.

This Janus-like ability to face simultaneously towards Europe and the US has of course been the cornerstone of British foreign policy in the modern era. In the context of space, the question is whether Britain can take advantage of its unique position by adopting a stronger leadership role in Europe, while at the same time steering the US away from a strategy based on total dominance towards one based on assurance.

So far there are few signs of this happening. In December 2002 Britain gave the US permission to upgrade its facilities at Fylingdales in Yorkshire, which are intended to form part of an eventual ground-based missile defence system. And on 12 June 2003 the US and UK signed a memorandum of understanding on missile defence. Questioned about this in the House of Commons, the defence secretary Geoff Hoon insisted that its contents 'remain confidential'.[52] It must be hoped that Britain is exerting pressure from behind closed doors. What US commentators such as Kagan fail to recognise is the extent to which the EU has created a model of open governance capable of sustaining deeper, longer-term forms of security. Britain is in a unique position to make this case.

When it comes to Britain's wider role in European space, there is also scope for more decisive leadership. The current ESA system encourages a flexible approach to investment – members pay a GDP-linked minimum subscription into a general pot, which funds ESA's core programme, and then countries choose to put extra funds into programmes they particularly support, or to opt out of those that they don't.

Britain is a past master at the flexible game. For example, it refuses to contribute to ESA's Ariane launcher programme, on the basis that it can get its satellites launched by Russia. It also likes to balance collaboration within ESA with plenty of bilateral working with NASA, on the assumption that this enables it to secure better leverage with both. However, there are signs that this classic British tactic is losing its efficacy. One industry insider told us that the US has in recent years chosen to work with Germany and France on a number of high-profile projects, in part because they are more fully at the heart of the European space programme.[53]

Perhaps surprisingly, Britain is most involved in those parts of ESA which are the most Venutian. It gives over the minimum contribution to environmental monitoring and has played a key role in ensuring ESA's leadership – both technical and political – in this area. This may offer a precedent for thinking differently about Britain's role in the European space programme. For Europe to fulfil Jean-Jacques Dordain's vision of space as a 'public good', a significant increase in space investment will be required. Europe needs to demonstrate that it is serious about distributing the benefits that space brings, in particular reducing the gap between the information-rich North and the information-poor South. On space and the environment, Britain has already carved out something of a leadership role within ESA. Could it now do the same around the international development agenda?

There is certainly some valuable expertise to draw on within the UK space community. One of the most innovative space companies is Surrey Satellites, an offshoot of Surrey University. In September 2003, it launched a constellation of small satellites to monitor natural disasters. Sir Martin Sweeting, Chief Executive, explains the rationale behind this cluster model:

> *Most conventional satellites only revisit the same site once every 10–20 days – so you could miss it completely. You need four to five satellites working together to give you 24-hour global coverage...We put together a consortium where each partner builds a satellite and then cooperatively owns and accesses all five satellites.*[54]

Algeria, China, Nigeria and Turkey have already signed up, and Surrey Satellites has been training teams in each country to operate the satellites. Colin Hicks, director-general of the BNSC, says that the project demonstrates how 'over the past twenty years, Britain has built up a world-leading position in small satellite technology'.[55]

Yet despite such bright spots of innovation, many do not regard

Figure 1: Space budgets as percentage of GDP in 2001

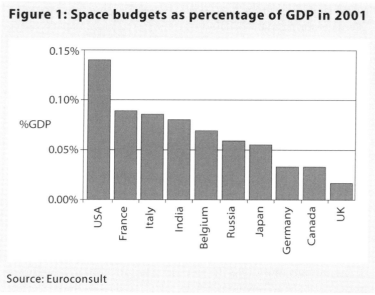

Source: Euroconsult

Britain as a space power of any significance. Comparisons of the proportion of GDP that different countries spend on space (military and civil) show how far we lag behind our international competitors. For the year 2001, the US spent 0.14 per cent of its GDP on space. France, Italy and India come in at around 0.09 per cent. The figure for Britain is a paltry 0.02 per cent. Even Belgium does better, with 0.07 per cent of its GDP spent on space (see Figure 1). The following chapter outlines the contribution that space can make to economy, society and environment; opportunities that Britain will miss out on unless it takes space a lot more seriously.

2. Intergalactic plumbing: space and the smart state

Imagine if we switched off space. Just for 24 hours. What difference would it make?

Penny Tranter would be one of the first to know. It's her job to present the weather four days a week on BBC 1. Most Mondays, she gets up at 7am and drives to work to start preparing the morning forecast. At the BBC Weather Centre she sits down in front of a bank of computers that hum and bleep as the latest satellite data flows in from the Met Office. Every hour the BBC receives a fresh batch of pictures of weather conditions across the UK. Penny knows that the data she receives is now so reliable that she will never do a 'Fishy forecast' – Weather Centre shorthand for the famous instance in 1987 when Michael Fish reassured viewers that all was well just hours before fierce storms swept across the country.

Except, of course, if space was switched off for a day. Then Penny would have a problem on her hands…

And she wouldn't be alone. Millions of people across the country would feel the effects. In the homes of BSkyB subscribers, TV screens would flicker and die. Out at sea, hundreds of ships would veer dangerously off course, struggling to navigate without their GPS systems. The flow of satellite data that underpins coastguard services, flood defences and environmental monitoring would dry up. In the far-flung corners of rural Britain, thousands of homes and businesses that rely on satellite for broadband internet access would be confronted with a 'service unavailable' message. A clutch of innovative e-health and e-learning projects would sputter to a halt. And, across the world, BBC, ITN and CNN reporters on assignment would be unable to transmit the latest pictures for the evening news.

Although many people remain unaware of them, space technologies are a vital part of the hidden infrastructure – the plumbing – of modern life. Satellite systems enable the networks of communication, navigation and monitoring that a growing proportion of public services and businesses depend upon. The government now aims to move this reliance up a level, by making the UK the world's 'most advanced user' of space services.[56]

Demos has written elsewhere about the challenges of creating a smart, 'adaptive state' that uses technology as an enabler of modernisation and renewal.[57] This chapter explores the role that space can play in improving the quality of the public realm. Analysing space from a purely economic perspective fails to capture the full contribution that it can make to wider social goods, such as broadband communication, public services and environmental sustainability.

There are many examples where this is already happening, or where the positive contribution of space is set to intensify over the next decade. Four areas are examined below: transport, broadband communication, location-based services and environmental science and protection.

Transport

Applications of satellite technology that have excited the most interest over the past year are in transport: specifically the use of GPS as the basis of a nationwide road pricing scheme. Now that Ken Livingstone has shown that congestion charging can work in London, the Department for Transport is considering the introduction of a national scheme. GPS offers the most effective method of doing this. By introducing a GPS 'black box' into every car, it would be possible to tax motorists for the precise distance travelled, and to vary charges according to time of day or location. So, a motorist travelling from

Birmingham to central London during rush hour would be charged a lot more than someone travelling on a rural road in the middle of the afternoon.

This system was recommended in 2002 by the government's transport watchdog, the Commission for Integrated Transport (CfIT).[58] The road lobby predictably attacked the proposal as a 'tax on motion', but CfIT suggested that its introduction be accompanied by an equivalent reduction in road tax and fuel duty, effectively making it revenue-neutral. Indeed, those drivers who own a car but use it comparatively little would actually be better off under the scheme.

The Department for Transport is now looking seriously at the options. There is ongoing debate as to whether revenue neutrality should be an objective, or whether road pricing needs to bite harder if it is to reduce congestion and transport-related pollution. A recent report from the Institute for Public Policy Research argues for the latter, suggesting that the scheme should aim to raise £16 billion per annum, which could then be ploughed back into public transport.[59]

Road pricing is only one of a variety of possible uses of GPS in transport. Thousands of drivers already use GPS as the basis of in-car navigation systems. And trial projects are also under way with public transport providers. For example, the Metroline bus company in London is using GPS to track all its buses and advise drivers to alter their speeds to avoid the well-known phenomenon of no buses turning up for 20 minutes, then three arriving at once.[60]

Case study: smart cabs

Londoners in need of a lift can now use Zingo, a service that matches customers to vacant licensed taxi cabs in the vicinity. The customer phones Zingo on their mobile phone and location-based technology then pinpoints their whereabouts, typically to within 500 metres. Using GPS, this information is sent to the nearest driver, who then speaks directly to the passenger to confirm their precise location. The service has not yet achieved pinpoint accuracy, but Zingo expects a combination of 3G mobile services and advances in GPS to sharpen its focus to within ten metres in the next few years.

Zingo has now expanded its service to cover 3,000 of London's 20,000 taxi cabs. The haphazard process of hailing cabs in the street may soon be redundant, and this system also has advantages in terms of personal security, by avoiding the safety hazards that are sometimes associated with unlicensed minicabs.

Digital Heineken

After a sluggish start, caused largely by BT's monopoly hold over the 'local loop', broadband has finally taken off in the UK.[61] Yet substantial swathes of rural Britain remain beyond the reach of broadband networks. BT has made strenuous efforts to extend access as widely as possible, but there is little economic case for wiring up remote and outlying areas, so a rump of between 5 and 10 per cent of the population is set to remain without broadband for the foreseeable future. Across Europe as a whole, that figure rises to as much as 20 per cent.[62]

This is where space comes in. Satellites have been described by one analyst as 'digital Heineken' – they refresh the parts of the broadband network that other providers cannot reach. The great advantage of satellite over terrestrial broadband is that it provides a very large 'footprint' of coverage without the cost of building local infrastructure. Already, a range of satellite services, such as Amba Broadband, is available in some parts of the country.

The downside is that satellite is an expensive option. It costs around £1,000 for installation and £50 per month for a subscription, compared with just £100 for installation and £25 per month for conventional ADSL services. These costs are falling, and some of the UK regional development agencies are supporting the 'Rabbit Initiative' (Remote Area Broadband Inclusion Initiative), which provides a subsidy of up to £700 towards installation and the first year of use.

There are also technical drawbacks: because of the distance that signals have to travel into space and back again, there is usually a short time-lag in transmission of around a quarter of a second. This isn't a problem if you are sending emails, but it makes online gaming – where rapid reactions are required – almost impossible. Satellite broadband also tends to slow down when a large number of users are relying on a single satellite connection. As Mark Main, senior analyst at Ovum observes: 'At times of peak internet usage, such as when there has been a virus, satellite internet quality degrades very quickly. It seems that when it is good it is very, very good, but when it is bad the service is appalling.'[63]

Nonetheless, there is no doubt that satellite broadband with some limitations is a lot better than no broadband at all, which is the choice confronting businesses and citizens in many rural areas in Britain and Europe.

Case study: mile-high broadband

Satellites could bring connectivity to other areas currently beyond the reach of the internet. In July 2003, the International Telecommunications Union agreed a frequency for high-speed internet access on aircraft. Boeing aims to have commercial services available in late 2004, with every passenger being guaranteed at least 156 kps of bandwidth on their flight. Andrew Weisheit, vice-president of Boeing subsdiary Connexion, explains how it works: 'It's the same technology that links terrestrial ATM machines. The difference is that our ATM machines are moving at 600 miles an hour.'

Beyond the EU, the potential is greater still. At the World Summit on the Information Society in December 2003, delegates were reminded of the scale of the global digital divide: 90 per cent of global internet users come from industrialised countries; Africa, which makes up 19 per cent of the world population, is home to only 1 per cent of internet users.[64] If connectivity in the developing world is to become widespread there is a need to leapfrog over fixed-line infrastructure straight to satellite or mobile networks. One of the reasons that satellite is so expensive in the UK is that there are already billions of pounds of investment sunk into the fixed-line alternatives. In large parts of Africa and Asia, hardly any of that infrastructure is in place, so satellite could work out as the most cost-effective and geographically flexible option.

Location, location, location

The potential of digital networks to facilitate more diverse, personalised and productive public services has been widely discussed.[65] Space technologies can play a part in this, most critically by supplying the navigation architecture for new location-based services. Whether through e-learning schemes or telemedicine, satellite systems offer an effective way to facilitate communication between different links in the public service chain. For example, to improve the links between hospital emergency departments and ambulance crews, European firm ITAL TBS is developing a tele-emergency service that will supply ambulances with full patient information through a GPS-guided system.[66]

Breakthroughs in mobile location-based services have been spurred by the miniaturisation of navigation systems. Over the past five years GPS units have shrunk from the size of an overhead projector to being able to fit inside a chip in a mobile phone. The Royal National Institute for the Blind has been quick off the mark in exploring how satellite navigation could transform the quality of life for the people it serves. Demos met the RNIB's chief scientist, Dr John Gill, who explained how:

> There are about one million people in the UK registered as blind or partially sighted…Many of these people are restricted to a limited number of standard routes that they've learnt and often don't have the information to connect up the routes or adapt them. I knew one woman who did her weekly shop using two standard routes. She walked from her house to one shop, back to her house, then walked to the next shop. The two shops were

next to each other, but she had no way of knowing this. GPS support systems offer a way to give blind and partially sighted people back their independence.[67]

John Gill and his team are investigating a number of GPS-assisted systems that use a combination of digital maps, photo-messaging and telephone support to provide users with real-time information and orientation. It is an idea that he thinks the government should be interested in:

> *The ageing population means that blindness and partial-sightedness are going to effect increasing numbers of people. A GPS system could prolong a person's independence and their mobility and that means delaying or even avoiding altogether going into long-term residential care.*

Case study: satellite surgeons

An innovative ESA-backed scheme developed by the University of Plymouth allows surgeons from 26 hospitals to take part in online training sessions. Footage of new surgical techniques is broadcast live via satellite from a TV studio in Plymouth and can be watched by trainee surgeons elsewhere. Direct interaction can also take place by phone, email or video conference. The programme saves time for students and surgical tutors, and allows new practices to be shared more rapidly.

Bridging the divide

Space-enabled services offer some of their best 'Heineken effects' outside the advanced industrial world. India is foremost among the developing countries that have recognised their value, and spending on India's civil space applications has increased fourfold since 1989. Kiran Karnik, head of Nasscom, India's main information technology industry association, explains: 'the guiding motive is to make technology that is useful for ordinary people in village India.'[68]

One of the areas being developed is telemedicine. Dr Devi Shetty is a strong candidate for the world's most regular tele-practitioner. In one year, Dr Shetty diagnosed and treated nearly 4,000 patients in isolated parts of India using satellite technology. He explains, 'India is a country where people still die because they cannot afford antibiotics or because they don't live anywhere near a medical centre. It is practically impossible to build one in every corner of rural India. Satellite technology helps bridge the gap.'[69]

Case study: international rescue

Reuter's AlertNet is the information one-stop shop for the international disaster relief community. The idea is to provide fast and reliable information and logistics to emergency relief charities operating in the field. It now has over 200 member charities and gets up to 1,000 hits a day. Demos met its editor, Mark Jones, who told us about the increasing role satellites were playing in helping to predict, respond and manage natural disasters across the globe – from flooding, earthquake damage and drought, to volcanic eruptions and severe weather. Powered by images supplied by ESA, the service offers a wealth of information that can be used to give early warning of some natural disasters and provide data about the size of floods, refugee camps and volcanic eruptions, as the basis for planning relief operations.

Green space

Right now, 500 miles above us, a satellite the size of a double decker bus is taking the pulse of the planet. Meet Envisat, the most sophisticated environmental monitoring device ever created.

Launched into orbit in March 2002, Envisat is now providing a steady stream of information to scientists back on Earth about the temperature of the oceans, the speed of winds and waves, the thickness of the ice sheets over Antarctica, and the pace of deforestation. With its battery of scientific instruments it can count plankton, detect pollution, and even warn of potential earthquakes and volcanic eruptions. Professor Alan O'Neill of Reading University is one of those receiving and interpreting the data. He likens Envisat to a 'body scanner' for Earth: 'We want to give the planet a real health check, to diagnose its state of health and offer a prognosis for the future.'[70]

Ask your average environmentalist how space can help in the quest for sustainability, and they will probably mutter darkly about money being wasted on shuttles that would have been better spent on solar power. There's little awareness of the contribution that space science is now making to our understanding of Earth's life support systems.

Yet what the green movement often forgets is the pivotal role that space played in awakening any kind of global environmental consciousness. Those early images of Earth, captured by the cameras of the Apollo programme, were for many a revelation of its beauty and delicate fragility. It is well known that James Lovelock was working as a NASA scientist when he first developed the Gaia hypothesis as a scientific response to this new way of seeing Earth.

Today, when versions of the Earth image are used on everything from credit cards to airline adverts, it is easy to forget what an impact those early pictures had. But as Sheila Jasanoff, professor of science and public policy at Harvard University, reminds us the Earth image has 'provided the chief impetus for environmental mobilization since the 1960s. It is a deeply political image…a fitting emblem of western environmentalism's transnational ambitions'.[71]

As Envisat shows, the symbolic contribution of space to environmental awareness is now being matched by a growing capacity for space to increase our understanding of how the planet works. The importance of space was formally recognised at the World Summit on Sustainable Development in 2002, which for the first time noted the contribution that space-based systems could make to sustainability. Further measures to share global environmental data were agreed in August 2003 at an Earth Observation Summit, hosted by US Secretary of State Colin Powell, and attended by more than 30 nations.

If we accept that we need the best possible science to underpin political and practical steps towards sustainability, space can play a vital role, particularly in obtaining data from remote or inaccessible parts of the world. For example, a team of scientists at University College London are using satellites to monitor ice flows in the Antarctic. Because they are able to survey vast areas, they can pinpoint particular glaciers that may be melting, and direct ground-based scientists towards them. Another team at the Centre for the Observation and Modelling of Earthquakes and Tectonics is using satellite technology to understand the secret life of earthquakes.

Steven Wilson of the Natural Environment Research Council sees new patterns of collaboration between space and ground-based science as the way forward: 'We are not interested in space *per se*. For us, it's a tool which allows us to do better environmental science. Using satellites in earth observation allows us to predict how things are changing, so ground-based research can be much more targeted.'[72]

It is not only the big global problems such as climate change that space can help us to understand. Satellites can also contribute to environmental knowledge at the local level. Earlier this year, a team at Reading University used space data to produce a gene-flow map for the UK, which revealed that GM oilseed rape, planted as part of the GM crop trials, was contaminating other crops.[73] In the Amazon region satellite pictures are being used by environmental groups such as World Resources Institute to map the changing pattern of deforestation; and in East Africa satellite data is now being used to track the size and spread of the gorilla population in the mountainous forests of Uganda and Rwanda, which are often impenetrable to ground-based scientists.

As José Achache, director of Earth Observation at the European Space Agency, explains, the value of space technology is that it enables policy-makers 'to operate at both the global and local level, and even more importantly, to couple these scales and move between them'.[74] Space technology can move between meta trends, such as tracking global rainfall changes, and micro trends, from tracing individual air pollutants to changes in land use.

In a sector where NASA is by far the biggest player, earth

monitoring is also a rare UK success story in space. We have more than our fair share of the world's leading scientists and are well placed to take a greater share of the European market for earth observation applications which was worth €216 million in 2000. The UK government contributed £300 million to the £1.4 billion costs of Enivisat, and 11 UK firms were involved in developing and building the satellite. Roger Sharpe, special adviser at the Department for Trade and Industry, argues that earth observation could form part of a wider drive for environmental innovation. 'Alongside green chemistry and carbon trading, it could become one of a basket of environmental technologies where the UK leads the world.'[75]

3. Stellar growth: innovation and the economics of space

Space is now a serious business. Worldwide, the space applications market is expected to be worth €350 billion a year by 2010.[76] Currently, in Europe, the space sector has an annual turnover of €5.5 billion, and directly employs 30,000 people. A new project such as Galileo is expected to generate €18 billion of benefits over 20 years.[77] In the UK, the BNSC estimates that the turnover of the upstream end of the space sector – primarily the manufacture of satellite systems – was £436 million. A further £2.5 billion was generated at the downstream end – mostly through communications, navigation and earth observation services.[78]

As new downstream applications are developed, the boundaries of the space sector expand, making precise measurement difficult. Yet one trend is clear: after 40 years in which governments and the military were the largest investors in space, emerging commercial markets are becoming the more significant sphere of economic opportunity. The OECD suggests that 'the space sector is now reaching a critical stage…more and more countries are seeking to take advantage of the opportunities that space may offer in the coming decades'.[79]

Today's space economy

Four main areas constitute the bulk of today's space economy.

Satellite communications

Over the past two decades satellite communications has become the largest area of commercial space activity and, despite the recent slump in telecoms investment, it is set to continue growing. Revenues reached $67 billion in 2000, driven by increased demand for communications bandwidth and convergence between broadband, multimedia, mobile and digital broadcast services. At the upstream end of the market, the failure of the low-orbit Iridium system and an excess of capacity have led to a few lean years for satellite manufacturers. Losses at EADS, Europe's largest satellite manufacturer and owner of EADS Astrium in the UK, reached €268 million in 2002. And European launcher efforts were dealt a further blow by the failure of the Ariane 5 rocket on its first mission in December 2002.

But with 26 launches scheduled for 2004, demand remains steady and is expected to pick up again in the second half of the decade. Downstream, demand for satellite services continues to grow steadily at around 17 per cent per annum. Direct-to-home television has enjoyed the fastest growth, with revenues of $9 billion in 2000.[80]

Launchers and transportation

Launch services also grew in the 1990s, accounting for around $5 billion most years. The US was the largest player in this market, but now faces stiff competition from Europe's Ariane programme and from a ready supply of cheaper launch vehicles from Russia, Ukraine and China. Since the cancellation of the Blue Streak rocket programme in the late 1960s the UK has not had any independent launch capacity, nor has it invested via ESA in the Ariane programme. Lord Sainsbury has repeatedly stated that the UK sees no commercial logic in spending money in this area, although this position was criticised during recent consultations on the UK space strategy. David Southwood, the director of science at ESA, sees the absence of a serious discussion of launchers in the UK strategy as a serious omission. In a set of comments to BNSC he asks: 'Is the array of present political launcher options not only commercially competitive but also politically satisfactory? Can the UK make strategic investments in activities like Galileo without a policy on independent access to space?'[81]

Looking to the future, most analysts believe that new launch technologies hold the key to growth. NASA is investing around $5 billion in this area through its Space Launch Initiative, but there are questions as to whether this will be sufficient when compared with the $40 billion that was required to develop the space shuttle. ESA is also working towards a successor to the Ariane programme through its Future Launch Technologies Programme. The alternative may be a radical innovation from smaller players at the margins of the industry. For example, David Ashford, the founder of Bristol Spaceplanes, argues that only a small amount of government investment is required to create a new generation of launchers capable of dramatically cutting satellite launch costs.[82]

GPS navigation

The market for satellite navigation services continues to enjoy robust growth at around 19 per cent per annum. In 2000 GPS-related revenues were over $7 billion, and as more products incorporate GPS chips, the prospects for the next few years are good.[83] GPS applications are diverse, ranging from military operations to mountaineering, car-based navigation to cardiac monitoring. Recreational and car-based systems are expected to grow fastest over the next five years, as the term 'GPS' becomes better known by the general public.

In the medium term the introduction of the superior Galileo system is expected to spur a shift away from US to European providers of location and navigation services, although given that Galileo will not become operational until 2008, this is unlikely to take real effect until the next decade. In the meantime, the US is planning to invest several billion dollars in modernising its existing system to improve its accuracy and reliability.[84]

Case study: pizza and chips

Domino's Pizza is teaming up with GPS experts Navman UK to ensure that cold, soggy pizzas become a thing of the past. By placing a small tracking chip in the shoe of all their delivery agents, Domino's will use GPS to make sure they reach the right address. As soon as the company takes an order, it will key the address into its main computer. This information will be sent to the chip in the shoe of the nearest driver, and a voice command giving directions will be transmitted from the shoe to a bluetooth headset.

Remote sensing

This is a younger market, which developed commercially from 1994 when the US decided to allow commercial firms to sell high-resolution images of Earth from space. The space analysts Futron estimate that the total market for remote sensing in 2000 was approximately $3.3 billion. Of this, raw satellite imagery (with no value-added interpretation) accounted for around $173 million. GIS (geographical information systems) software accounted for around $1.2 billion. There has been a rush of new entrants to this market in the past few years and, as the cost of services falls, most analysts predict that the market will grow significantly, provided a greater number of users or intermediaries develop the necessary skills to interpret imaging data.[85]

Long waves of innovation

If these are the space markets of today, what new markets will develop over the next 10 or 20 years? And what contribution could space make to the wider challenges of improving UK productivity and competitiveness?

Michael Porter, in his recent study of UK productivity for the DTI, describes the three stages that nations go through in developing their competitive advantages. The first is the *factor-driven stage*, in which competitiveness is based on low-wage labour and natural resources. The second is the *investment-driven stage*, in which efficiency in production and outsourcing become the dominant source of advantage. The third stage is the *innovation-driven stage*, when the ability to develop innovative products and services at the frontier of new technology becomes the key to competitiveness.

Despite improvements in UK productivity over the past 20 years, Porter argues that the UK now sits at the 'transition point' between the second and third stages: 'Competing on relatively low input costs and an efficient business environment is no longer sufficient to achieve the levels of prosperity the country is aiming for…UK companies will need to upgrade their productivity by competing on more unique and more innovative products and services.'[86]

The economists Chris Freeman and Francisco Louca offer an historical perspective that complements Porter's analysis. They suggest that over the past two centuries five technological revolutions have successively transformed the societies in which they were developed. These revolutions – water-powered mechanisation, steam-powered mechanisation, electrification, motorisation and computerisation – can be understood as '*long waves*' of innovation, growth and institutional change, which diffuse over time.[87]

When clusters of technological innovations form disruptive constellations they generate a paradigmatic shift in the overall trajectory of a society. For example, the combination of copper, steel and electricity combined to transform the socioeconomic landscape of the nineteenth century in ways that would have been entirely unpredictable when Cruickshank's primary battery was invented in 1800. The challenge is to understand how these disruptive constellations emerge, spread and ultimately come to dominate economic and social systems, before giving way to the next constellation.

An important distinction that this long wave theory helps to lay bare is that between *disruptive* and *incremental* innovation.

Incremental innovation

Incremental innovation is a continuous process of making small improvements in efficiency and performance within the fixed parameters of a product, business model, institution or social practice. Rather than investing in innovations that may ultimately supersede existing products, services or ways of working, incremental innovation means eking out as much advantage as possible from existing operations. Examples of this would be a 'new and improved' recipe of a successful breakfast cereal, marginal improvements in a school's attendance record, or allowing tax returns to be completed online. Another good example is the way that cars have gradually become more aerodynamic, fuel-efficient and comfortable, while their basic engine technology, shape and structure have changed little in 60 years.

Disruptive innovation

Disruptive innovation produces changes of an entirely different order; a product, business model or organisational system that changes an entire field of practice. Disruptive innovation in management methods, for example, led to the lean production system pioneered by Toyota and subsequently adopted across the entire automotive industry. Disruptive innovations tend to transform the landscape within which organisations operate, disrespecting traditional methods and products. Examples include Microsoft's Windows operating system, Ikea's impact on the furniture market or Amazon's approach to book retailing. In another sphere, the use of ICTs to facilitate home-based medical and respite care might eventually cause massive disruption to the organisation of primary healthcare and hospitals.

In his book *The Innovator's Dilemma* Clayton Christensen identifies several key characteristics of disruptive innovation:

○ They tend to emerge from seemingly insignificant markets.
○ They initially underperform against market-leading products and brands.
○ Few consumers want or think they need the new product or application.
○ They squeeze the profit margins of the older order.[88]

This is why it is often difficult for companies or governments to anticipate the eventual value of disruptive innovations. A good example is the mobile phone, which many people were deeply sceptical about when it was first launched. Now those same people find it hard to imagine life without one. This unpredictability hampers willingness to invest in risky new technologies, applications and services. The consequences of being risk averse only become apparent when the new innovation arrives. Organisations find themselves taken by surprise and have to embark on a painful period of adjustment.

Disruptive space?

Looking across the landscape of existing and emerging space technologies it is interesting to consider which of these have been – or have the potential to become – genuinely disruptive. Arguably the leading candidate is the satellite. By removing the geographical and temporal barriers to communication and enabling connectivity between any two points on the globe, satellites have enabled a host of applications in telecoms, broadcasting navigation and earth monitoring, the full effects of which are still playing out.

Of these satellite applications, GPS also stands out as a disruptive innovation, which has altered sectors and activities such as aviation, shipping and mountaineering. Within the next decade, it looks set to have a similar impact on road transport if satellite boxes are fixed in every car. Galileo may appear to offer only an incremental advance on GPS, but the openness of Galileo's protocols may also give rise to unexpected innovations.

The core question now confronting the space industry is how to identify and spread new sources of innovation. At various points in the past 40 years – most notably in the Apollo era – the space industry was perceived as a hotbed of ingenuity and scientific excellence. This reputation has waned in recent years, in part because the impacts of space technology are less visible, and also because the industry has failed to sustain a flow of innovative products and services. Indeed, unless it can rediscover some of its dynamism, the space industry is in danger of slipping into a *crisis of creativity*, compounded by its ageing workforce.

Part of the problem is the unusually high barriers to new entrants in space. Space is a hostile and risky environment to work in. Massive amounts of upfront capital are required and the market is highly cyclical, with complex interdependencies between the civil and defence markets. Yet, despite all of these challenges, there are a number of exciting areas of potential – some close to market, others further away in the future. A recent report for the US Department of Commerce conveys this sense of possibility:

> *Some envision a day when space will be a place for tourism, complete with hotels and cruise ships, and industries will also thrive in orbit, with research labs and manufacturing plants taking advantage of the microgravity environment. In such a future vision, movies will be filmed in space; unimagined sporting events will be played there; advertisers will flood the new environment with their messages; and space platforms will generate energy for people on earth.*[89]

Are such predictions the stuff of science fiction, or do they represent a genuine economic opportunity? Below we survey the potential of three longer-term markets: space tourism, space gaming, logistics and microgravity.

Space tourism

> *There are no ordinary people in space. Space needs to be more fun.*
>
> Rachel Armstrong[90]

Space and the entertainment industry have long enjoyed a close association. But so far the relationship has been rather one-sided, with the adventure of space providing a high-octane fuel for box office receipts. Seven out of the 20 biggest grossing films of all time have a space theme, with *Armageddon* alone making over $800m at the box office. Some of the economic potential for the space industry over the next 20 years lies in claiming back some of this value, and using the adventure, excitement and exploration associated with space as the basis of new services. The Republican Congressional candidate in Alabama, Michael Williams, has proposed one way of doing this: imposing a 1 per cent 'Star Trek tax' on all space-related books, films and toys. However, there are much easier ways of creating value from space. Foremost among them is space tourism, an industry that is about to enter the mainstream.

Tourism is now the world's largest industry, employing approximately 10 per cent of the world's working population, and with a total turnover predicted to reach $2,000 billion by 2020.[91] Integral to the tourist experience is the pursuit of novelty. Within this picture of overall growth, one of the fastest-growing sectors is adventure travel and leisure, with people pursuing increasingly adrenalin-rich activities, from rock-climbing and mountaineering to skydiving and free-diving. But with almost every inch of the globe mapped by Lonely Planet and Baedekers, new sources of novelty are constantly being sought. Entertainment and tourism have the potential to become a new focus for the space industry, in the way that the military was in the past. As Sir Martin Sweeting of Surrey Satellites explained to us, already 'the biggest investments and advances are in leisure technology, not the military...We go and get the latest thing from Sony and stick it on one of our spacecraft.'[92]

Space has always been the exclusive domain of nation states, but in 2001 Dennis Tito broke this monopoly. He spent $20 million on a ticket on a Russian rocket and a mini-break at one of the galaxy's more unusual hotels: the International Space Station, 240 miles above Earth. Shortly afterwards, Mark Shuttleworth became the second tourist to enter space. This signals a revolution in access to space, as NASA has itself recognised: 'Now the dream of very many of us during the Apollo era that we could sometime take a trip to space for our own personal reasons is finally approaching realisation...this is fundamentally a new dimension of space that can and should be created.'[93]

Analysts have been trying to forecast the potential size of the space tourism market for more than a decade. The most sophisticated study to date suggests that at a price of $400,000 a ticket, 10,000 passengers each year would purchase a trip to space, creating a $4 billion annual market.[94]

And of course, the appetite for space adventures already exists. Cape Canaveral in Florida is a well-established fixture on the tourist trail, competing alongside Disney. WildWings, a UK adventure holiday firm, offers various space-based experiences that are available now, including a supersonic jet flight to the edge of space for £8,125 and zero-gravity adventures in parabolic flight aircraft for £3,485. Looking to the future, the architect firm Wimberley Allison Tong and Goo have designed an orbiting space hotel catering for 100 guests, which they suggest could be up and running by 2017. And the Hilton International chain has announced its intention to be the first hotelier on , commissioning architect Peter Inston to come up with the design. His colossal 5,000-room dome structure would run off solar energy and water from the lunar ice.

The first step to realising the potential of full-scale space tourism is developing a viable market for sub-orbital flights. Serious efforts to do this are now being led by a diverse group of private companies, space enthusiasts and wealthy individuals. Their goal is to create the first commercial reusable spacecraft. Just as the Orteig Prize and Charles Lindbergh's non-stop flight between New York and Paris in 1927 spurred the development of faster, cheaper and safer commercial flying, the $10m 'X-prize' is now up for grabs to any private organisation that succeeds in launching a vehicle capable of carrying three people 100km up and down twice in two weeks. There are 23 teams from around the world competing, with Burt Rutan from California the current favourite. The US-based company Space Adventures is already taking bookings for sub-orbital flights, which it hopes to commence as early as 2005. They have already received over 140 deposits.[95]

So far governments have shown a persistent lack of interest in making lower-cost access to space available to the public. NASA, keen to preserve existing budgets for the Shuttle, is reluctant to support the development of fully reusable spaceplanes. The potential environmental impacts of space tourism are also held up as a sensible reason not to proceed far in this direction.

However, with the promise of reducing the flight time from London to Sydney to just 75 minutes, sub-orbital space planes cannot be entirely written off. They may yet come to be a defining space innovation of the twenty-first century.

The virtual universe

15 years from now...Internet connections may cover our solar system and many people could be controlling their own robots on different planets.

Anders Hansson, director, European Institute
of Quantum Computing[96]

While most attention has focused on flying people to the stars, arguably the greater potential lies in virtual forms of tourism. Space has always been the ultimate spectator sport. The 1969 Apollo moon landing was one of the first global television events. The rivalry between the US and the Soviet Union even provided people with teams to root for. Now, the way is open for space to become a *participation* sport. Capitalising on developments in robotics and quantum computing, we may not need to leave Earth to enjoy the spectacle of extra-terrestrial tourism. Virtual tourism opens the ways for the public to become explorers, not just passengers, and all at a much lower cost and with much less of a negative environmental impact.

The rise of the gaming industry gives an indication of the size of the market for virtual adventuring. Globally, 30 million Play Station 2, X-box and Games cube consuls were sold in 2002. In the UK alone the gaming market was worth over £1 billion in 2003. The potential appetite for virtual adventuring can be gauged by the popularity of the most participative space missions so far. In 1997 NASA's Pathfinder robot rover landed on Mars and beamed back images to Earth, which were then distributed on the internet. The mission gave an unprecedented sense of immediacy and intimacy, letting viewers see Mars through the rover's eyes. The Pathfinder website received over half a billion hits in its first month just for a series of still photographs. Six years later, NASA's Spirit rover is beaming back TV quality colour pictures of Mars. In the 24 hours after Spirit landed NASA recorded 109 million hits on its home page.[97]

Virtual adventuring could be developed in two ways. First, by using high-resolution satellite technology to create stored data-sets of entire planets. Using advances in virtual reality technology, entire land-scapes from Mars to Venus could be made available for exploration. Second, remote robots could be deployed to provide real-time interactivity. Users could control the direction of the robot and experience a variety of sensory inputs including digital quality video, surround sound, motion, temperature changes and even smell.[98] The possibilities are enormous. As John Taylor, director-general of the UK Research Councils told us, 'this offers one way for millions of people to enjoy the possibilities of space.' For the more timid, there would be guided rambles on the Moon; for the more adventurous, solo treks to the top of Olympus Mons, the 24km-high volcano on Mars.[99]

A number of companies are beginning to explore these oppor-tunities, for example www.exploremarsnow.com. One of the most advanced is LunarCorp, which, in conjunction with the Robotics Institute at Carnegie Mellon University, is developing a series of space-based adventures. In 2004 LunarCorp plans to launch its own SuperSat Lunar Orbiter, the first broadband space probe able to beam back high-speed, high-quality digital video using a 25 mbps communications channel. This capability will be used to map to the highest resolution yet and provide panospheric video images that will capture the view from the SuperSat in every direction. The data will then be pumped into specially developed telepresence portals located at science centres and theme parks, generating a totally immersive environment for users. 'Visitors will be able to turn in any direction to see the view from the spacecraft, as though they were floating alongside it in outer space. They'll be able to look down at the Moon whizzing by below, back towards the blue Earth or out into the solar system.'[100]

LunarCorp also plans to send an interactive rover to the Moon's surface, again using telepresence technology. 'Visitors will feel every dip into a crater or bump over a rock...They'll hear the groan of the motors and the crunch of the wheels on lunar dirt...They'll feel the chill in the air. And they will gaze out over the lunar surface with digital clarity, seeing it with the sharpness of an Apollo astronaut standing on the Sea of Tranquillity.'[101]

Microgravity

The zero-gravity conditions of space offer distinctive opportunities for certain types of experiments. For example, crystals grow larger and with less structural flaws, and cell growth occurs differently. This has led to speculation about the larger-scale potential of conducting scientific research, or eventually manufacturing, in a microgravity environment. One of the main arguments for constructing the International Space Station was that it would enable such experiments to be carried out over time. The UK is not involved in the International Space Station, but does participate in ESA's more modest microgravity programme.

One of the most interesting areas for microgravity is medical research. Dr Kevin Fong has introduced the first undergraduate course in space medicine and physiology at University College London. He explained to us what motivated his work: 'Studying science at the extremes can tell us a lot. I am interested in doing the same for the human body. What happens if you take a human being and put them in space, at the very edge of their survival curve?'[102] Researchers studying the human body in space are hopeful that the data will be of direct benefit back on Earth, for example in improving intensive care treatment and overcoming muscle wastage in patients affected by prolonged hospital-bed treatment – a problem shared by astronauts in zero-gravity conditions.

So far, the private sector has not begun to explore seriously the opportunities of conducting research in a microgravity environment, but over the next decade it may become a viable option for biotechnology, pharmaceutical and semiconductor companies. It would only take one or two scientific breakthroughs in this environment for microgravity to develop rapidly.

Experimentation matters

As Clayton Christensen argues in his new book, *The Innovator's Solution*, the challenge is to get to the other side of the innovator's dilemma, to create disruptions rather than be destroyed by them. The areas described above are not the only ones that could give rise to the disruptive innovations that will be key to the future success of the space industry. The UK space industry needs to decide where to focus its efforts for the next decade. In a global market, it cannot expect to compete in more than a handful of key areas, an assumption on which the government's space strategy is based. Based on today's strengths, key areas of opportunity for the UK over the next decade are likely to remain small satellites, earth observation and astrobiology.

But it is also worth bearing in mind the example of Nokia, which transformed itself in less than a decade from a company producing rubber boots to the leading light of the mobile age. The lesson is that in new technology markets you *can* move from nowhere to the lead with the right mixture of risk-taking and investment. An interesting question to pose for the next decade is who will be the Nokia of space? Could the same path of disruptive innovation be followed by a UK company in creating reusable spaceplanes? Such a gamble may not occur in the larger space nations, such as the US and France, which have invested so heavily in conventional space hardware. It could be a new entrant, like China, India or Malaysia, that leapfrogs to the next generation of technology. But the UK could also play a part. Its decision, much lamented by many in the space community, to pull out of conventional launch vehicles in the 1960s could turn out to be a blessing. It at least means that the UK has no vested interest in maintaining conventional space hardware, and can think more creatively about new technologies and services in space.

4. To boldly go? Space science and the quest for life

For the past six years, from the comfort of their living rooms, thousands of people have been engaged in an unlikely pursuit: the hunt for alien life. SETI@home is the world's largest distributed science experiment. With 4 million citizen-astronauts spread across 200 countries, it represents a pioneering example of 'open source' science. Like the communities of hackers and programmers that have helped to create the Linux operating system, SETI@home shows how distributed models of organisation and knowledge creation are often the most effective.

SETI@home stands for the 'Search for Extra-Terrestrial Intelligence at Home'. Run out of UC Berkeley, it is a free scheme, which encourages people to install a screensaver and programme on to their personal computer. The PC then devotes any idle processing capacity to analysing radio signals from outer space for signs of intelligent life. No aliens have been encountered yet, but SETI@home offers a glimpse of a new type of space science: one that places openness and public participation centre-stage.

The appliance of science

Space science seeks to answer the most fundamental questions of existence. Not only 'how did we get here?' and 'are we alone?', but even 'how did *everything* get here?' There is an emerging consensus among leading scientists that advances in our capacity to explore and analyse the Universe mean that these questions could be answered over the next decade.

The most exciting potential discovery is some kind of proof of extra-terrestrial life. Scientific optimism in this regard has been triggered by a series of discoveries in recent years. First, that there are a diversity of environments in our own solar system, including ice on the Moon and Mars and the possibility of water on one of Saturn's moons. Second, the discovery of about 120 new planets in our own galaxy, which greatly multiplies the potential sites for life. Third, back on Earth, the discovery that life can exist in hostile environments that scientists had previously thought impossible. These *extremophile* micro-organisms have been found to be living in places including nuclear reactors, hundreds of metres inside rock without any oxygen, and deep at the bottom of the ocean.

Laurence Bergreen argues that this these discoveries have created a paradigm shift in astrobiology, the science of extra-terrestrial life. He describes this shift as follows:[103]

Old paradigm	*New paradigm*
Intelligent, exotic aliens	Extremophile, microbial life
Purposeful	Random
Distant	Could be located on the next planet
A fluke of nature	Inevitable outcome of chemistry
Contains spiritual implications	Confirms accepted scientific theories
Scarce	Widespread
Requires Earth-like environment	Can develop in environments different from those found on Earth

Life on Mars

Humans have long looked at Mars and speculated about its life-bearing properties. In the 1890s Percival Lovell believed that he had identified a network of Martian-made canals across the planet's surface. Until 40 years ago many scientists believed that Mars was covered with thick vegetation. These myths were finally dispelled in the late 1960s when NASA's Mariner 6 and 7 flew past the planet and sent back the first images of a barren landscape. NASA's Viking Missions in 1976 seemed to confirm that Mars was indeed lifeless.

But now the bets are on that Mars could be home to the holy grail of astrobiology. In the late 1990s the Mars Global Surveyor provided the strongest evidence yet that Mars was once a warm and wet planet and could have provided the right conditions for life. Evidence of the hardiness of extremophiles on Earth means there is even a chance that some kind of microbial life is still living deep in the Martian rock. Alternatively, it could be that life moved between Earth and Mars, catching a ride on the turbulent shower of meteorites that bombarded both planets during the early years of the Universe. If the latter is true, we may yet discover that we are all in fact Martians.[104]

The Beagle 2 mission offered a good chance to learn whether there ever was life on Mars. Had the mission succeeded, its on-board equipment would have drilled below the surface to analyse soil samples for chemical traces of life. NASA's Spirit and Opportunity landers may also uncover signs of life, although they lack the sophisticated instruments of Beagle. If no conclusive evidence is found, it may be necessary to wait for the next round of Mars missions, scheduled for 2009. Unless of course Colin Pillinger can get Beagle 3 off the ground any earlier.

Looking for Earth-like planets

With half-a-trillion stars in the Milky Way and at least 10 billion billion in the observable universe, it seems improbable that only one supports life. Over the past decade, around 120 new planets have been spotted orbiting other stars. However, the only ones detected so far are extremely large – at least the size of Jupiter – which are thought to be unsuitable for life. To spot smaller 'habitable' planets (rocky ones that are capable of developing and retaining an atmosphere) we need to journey deeper into space.

Over the next 15 years Europe is going to be at the forefront of this search, with a trio of habitable planet hunters being launched. In 2008 the Eddington probe will begin a survey of 500,000 stars in the Milky Way, which scientists believe will lead to the detection of around 100 Earth-like planets in the so-called Goldilocks zone, the region around a star that has the best chance of supporting life because it is neither too hot nor too cold. In 2012 the Gaia probe will pick up the hunt, surveying the nearest billion stars. And pencilled in for around 2015 is Darwin, with its flotilla of eight spacecraft flying in formation. Darwin will detect light from Earth-like planets and analyse the chemical compositions of distant atmospheres, searching for the telltale chemical signs of life.

Just what is existence?

One of the greatest mystery currently occupying astronomers is understanding what the bulk of the Universe is made of. Gerry Gilmore, Professor of Experimental Philosophy at the Institute of Astronomy at Cambridge University, explained the puzzle to us:

> I've weighed the Milky Way and worked out its total weight. The problem is that everything we can see, from Earth, our sun and the other planets to the most distant stars, only account for about 3 per cent of that weight. I am now trying to work out what the other 97 per cent is ..People have a few hunches, but the only way to describe it for now is 'existence'.[105]

Others have termed this 'dark matter'. However labelled, it represents a dramatic extension to the series of revolutions that have successively shifted human understanding of our position in the Universe since Copernicus in the sixteenth century. The race is now on to find out what the rest of existence consists of. Scientists are confident that the dark matter mystery will be resolved in the next 20 years – a great leap forward in understanding the structure of the Universe.

UK scientists are also active at another edge of science, by looking back in time to the first second after the big bang. New techniques are being developed to trace this violent event by detecting the gravitational waves it generated. Andrew le Masurier of PPARC explained the idea to us: 'These waves, which are minute ripples in the fabric of space-time, travel across the Universe at the speed of light unaffected by intervening matter. They carry information about their origin, and by analysing them scientists might for the first time be able to see right back to the big bang itself.'[106]

The problem is that these waves are extremely faint. The only way to pick up the big bang's waves is by building detectors millions of kilometres long. UK scientists are trying to tackle this technological challenge. The SMART 2 mission, which will be launched in 2006, will test run some of the technologies. In 2012 the first full-blown space-based gravitational wave detector will be launched – the Laser Interferometer Space Antenna (LISA). This mission will consist of three spacecraft, each separated from the other two by 5 million kilometres. Laser beams will be sent between the spacecraft and the passage of gravitational waves detected by looking for slight changes in the interference pattern where the beams combine.

From human space to open space

Across the space community, at conferences, in books and on websites, there are frequent calls for the UK government to invest in human space flight. Supporters of human exploration argue that it provides unique insights into the Universe, and provides the best means of sustaining public and political support for space. A recent essay by Adam Keiper summarises this view:

> We all appreciate the pictures sent back from the Hubble telescope and our little robotic friends on Mars, but the inspirational stuff is in the human story, the adventure of space...We think of the Moon: the first steps, the flags, the golf balls. We think of Apollo 13, and the three lucky men who survived that mission...We think of the joy of weightlessness, and we think of the pain of loss: Apollo 1, Challenger, Columbia.[107]

Critics of human exploration point out that it is expensive, dangerous and can provide answers to very few of the questions that are currently occupying space science. While the costs of human space flight escalate, robotic probes are becoming smaller, faster and cheaper. NASA maintains an almost equal allocation of resources to human and robotic space – each accounting for around $8 billion a year. But the UK's position is clear. It is the only fully fledged space nation and member of the European Space Agency that invests absolutely nothing in human space flight. This is news to the British public: our MORI poll found that 47 per cent of respondents believe the UK is currently involved in human space, and 55 per cent believe it should become more involved.

Contrary to these poll findings, our view is that the UK government is right to focus its limited budget in other areas of space science and technology. Too often astronauts are portrayed as a magic solution to all the problems of the space industry. Yet the reality is that even during the height of the Apollo era, human space flight failed to maintain the interest of the public. By the time of Apollo 17 in 1972, NASA was paying TV networks to cover the mission. The myth of human space missions automatically having greater public appeal was also reflected in our MORI poll, which found that while 55 per cent of people polled thought Britain should be involved in human space missions, 65 per cent thought Britain should be involved in robotic missions.

Debates about human exploration can also act as a distraction from the more immediate challenge of strengthening public engagement in space through more open models of space science, of which SETI@home is a good example. There is a need to move beyond a *representative* model of public participation – the astronaut heading off into the sky as a token representative of the human race – towards a *distributed* model of participation – with as many people as possible becoming actively involved in the goals and activities of space science. The latent interest of the public is there; space science must tap into this and turn it to its advantage.

Within broader debates about science and society, the past five years have seen a shift away from a deficit model based around the 'public understanding of science' to a more participatory model of public engagement.[108] The space community needs to keep pace with this shift, which has profound implications for the techniques that it uses to engage with the public. At the moment, too many voices within the space community are still harking back to a deficit model, by portraying the public's ignorance or lack of enthusiasm for space as the source of the problem. Human space exploration is often advocated or defended in this light – of value insofar as it excites people about space, even if the underlying scientific argument for doing it is weak.

Any long-term strategy aimed at building public support for space has to be built on more solid foundations. It has to start from a recognition that public disillusion or lack of enthusiasm for space is one manifestation of a wider governance gap that has opened up between science and the rest of society. Crude attempts to bridge this gap using astronauts are doomed to failure. If first-rate space science is best achieved through robotic missions, it is pointless – not to mention irresponsibly wasteful of the limited resources available for space – to call in the short term for more human exploration. Instead, the key must be finding new ways to engage people in a wider range of processes and choices surrounding space science. Space scientists should capitalise on the existing levels of public interest in their work by evolving new models of 'open innovation' – which give interested members of the public a genuine stake in the direction and outcomes of their work. If over the long term a case for human exploration develops, then it should be judged purely on its scientific and economic merits.

This is another area of tension between US and European visions for space. At precisely the time that the space community should be embracing new forms of open innovation, President Bush's announcement of a massive boost in funding for human exploration, combined with his enthusiasm for weaponisation, has sent a strong signal that the US favours a closed approach. Whether or not NASA continues to outspend the rest of the world in space, it is this bias towards closed systems and against openness that is likely to weaken US dominance in space over the longer term.

Aurora: putting the European vision into practice

Of all the European projects proposed for the next 20 years, the one that is now generating the most excitement is Aurora. This will be a phased programme, starting with a series of robotic missions to the Moon and to Mars, and culminating in a human mission to Mars around 2030. The first half of the programme, which will run until at least 2015, will have a strong focus on astrobiology and life sciences. In the second phase, the emphasis will shift towards human exploration.

In this sense, Aurora is both tantalising and frustrating. The first half of the programme is expected to feature some of the most ambitious and ground-breaking robotic missions ever attempted. As part of this, Colin Pillinger will be able to bid for a Beagle 3 mission that uses even more sophisticated technologies than Beagle 2. The initial response to Aurora from the space community has been overwhelming. So far, 580 scientists from 30 countries have submitted proposals for instruments to be included on Aurora's ExoMars mission, which is due to be launched in 2009.[109]

Yet in the second half of the programme ESA is proposing to play catch-up with NASA, by joining the race to put astronauts on Mars. The strategic rationale for this is flimsy at best. ESA argues that certain scientific experiments are best conducted by humans rather than robots, but it seems doubtful that these benefits will justify the potential for this half of the programme to absorb such a huge amount of money. The other argument being made is the familiar and unsubstantiated claim that this will somehow re-engage the public in space. However, as we argue above, there are many more innovative and genuinely participative methods of achieving this objective. Furthermore, at a practical level, ESA will struggle to compete with NASA's deeper pockets and greater experience in human exploration.

So our conclusions are a hearty yes to phase one of Aurora, but a polite no to phase two. At the moment, the UK is hovering on the sidelines of the programme and has not yet made a decision to commit to the programme. We believe there is a strong case for the UK to take an early lead by committing the necessary resources for phase one – estimated at around £25 million a year for five years. This view is supported by our MORI poll, which found that 75 per cent of respondents believe the UK should join Aurora, compared with only 27 per cent who see it as a waste of money. However, 78 per cent said that they would want more information about Aurora before the government commits money to the programme.

As for the human exploration element of Aurora, our argument is that it makes far more sense for Europe to concentrate on its existing strengths in space, and areas of growing potential such as astrobiology and earth observation. The US is welcome to invest its energies and its taxpayers' money in trying to send humans to Mars. In the meantime, let Europe forge ahead in solving the remaining mysteries of the Universe.

5. Rocket dreams: space and our social imagination

French artist Jean-Marc Philippe is busy constructing the definitive message in a bottle. He plans to launch a spacecraft that will have a computer memory large enough to bank a message from all of the 6 billion people on Earth. The spacecraft will then orbit the Earth for 5,000 years. His plan stands in sharp contrast with the usual nation state model of space – the expert astronaut charged with a 'flag and footprints' mission. But space is changing, and so too is its relationship with society.

Ever since people began contemplating the stars, space has played an important role in our social imagination. The fascination stretches from at least the second century AD when the Greek philosopher Lucian of Samosata wrote two odysseys where his characters travelled to the Moon.[110] The hold that space has on our collective consciousness has persisted to a large extent because of its ability to appeal to a wide range of human aspirations. The Apollo era can be seen as a high point of this trend, helping to propel space to the forefront of media, political and societal agendas. However, a gap has now grown between the cultural symbols that government and industry space programmes project and the aspirations and values of wider society.

This chapter examines the changing cultural power of space, why the Apollo years cannot be recreated, and how space can reconnect with society by tapping into new forms of public imagination.

The Apollo years

The Apollo programme spoke very directly to the human aspiration to explore. Willie Ley, one of the early advocates of space travel, explains:

> *It is the story of a great idea, a great dream, if you wish, which probably began many centuries ago on the islands off the coast of Greece. It has been dreamt again and again ever since…It is the story of the idea that we possibly could, and if so we should, break away from our planet and go exploring to others, just as thousands of years ago men broke away from their islands and went exploring to other coasts.*[111]

Space travel arrived just in time to maintain the dream of exploration. Alaska, the polar regions and the Himalayas were all well mapped by the mid-1930s. The only way explorers could go was up. While the exploration ideal appealed to many countries, in the US it combined with another potent force – the myth of the national frontier. First made popular by the historian Frederick Turner in the 1890s, and romanticised through hundreds of Hollywood films, this myth claims that many distinctive qualities in American society, including optimism, individualism and inventiveness, derive from having free land across an open frontier.

In an interview with Demos, space advocate Robert Zubrin called this 'frontier shock' and described it as 'the most powerful harbinger of human progress'.[112] It is no coincidence that many of the space art paintings of Mars and other extra-terrestrial destinations look remarkably like the American 'Wild West'. Notions of frontier were critical in determining what kind of space programme emerged in the US – one that emphasised the centrality of humans to the exploration quest.

The power of the space programme in the Apollo years was not just its ability to reflect back the aspirations of society. It went a step further, with space becoming part of popular culture itself. The launch of Sputnik in 1957 triggered what Sean Topham describes as a craze for the futuristic, which lasted through to the early 1970s.[113] There was an explosion of space images on the packaging of all kinds of consumer products, such as the Smash robots used to sell instant mashed potato.

The race to the Moon contributed to a wider cultural atmosphere of experimentation, which combined with a set of cheap and malleable man-made materials to give rise to 'the space-age look'. Taking their inspiration from the styling of satellites and spacecraft, zero-gravity living and astronaut suits, designers began producing for the space-age consumer. Eero Aarnio's suspended 'Bubble Chair' (1967), John Lautner's 'Chemosphere', a flying-saucer-shaped house (1960), Colin Brignall's 'Countdown' typeface (1965) and André Courrèges's 'Cosmos' clothing collection (1967) typified this new age.[114]

The space programme reinforced some of the messages of the new consumer culture. It was the ultimate manifestation of the throwaway society, with millions of dollars invested into rockets, such as Titan 3 and Saturn V, to be just used once. Howard McCurdy argues that the space programme represents the most dramatic manifestation of the tendency in modern capitalism for 'other-directed' activity. The Apollo programme was the definitive status symbol which America used to convince other nations of its worth as it competed for their Cold War allegiance.[115]

Mind the gap

Today, the space age no longer feels like the future. It doesn't even feel like the present. There are a number of explanations for this. First, the frontier myth has lost much of its power. Since the Apollo era it has been subject to much revision and critique, especially surrounding the negative experiences of Native Americans, African Americans and women. The space programme itself has increasing failed to represent a changing society, a point made by Gill Scott Heron in his song 'Whitey on the Moon'. For many people, frontiers have come to mean conquest, rather than progress.

Second, there has been a loss of faith in a model of linear progress driven by technology. The early optimism and confidence of the consumer age has been undermined by doubts about its sustainability and spiritual hollowness. Technology is no longer seen as inevitably benign, as the highly contested debates around biotechnology and nanotechnology highlight. Equally, the deeply gendered language of space technology and exploration, a product of the dominance of men in the industry, further distances it from many people's experience of society.

Third, a gap has grown between the popular image of space and the reality of government space programmes. The US reached the Moon within a decade of Kennedy declaring it his goal. This set the pace for what people expected to follow. But 40 years later there are no Moon colonies, humans on Mars or space hotels. The reality of space has become routine and familiar, thus losing much of its capacity to engage and entertain. NASA has perpetuated this gap by continuing to promote a vision of space exploration that is full of space colonies and trips to Mars while at the same time failing to invest sufficient resources to make any of these visions real.

Marina Benjamin has described this as the split between the 'real NASA' and 'paper NASA'. Real NASA builds and operates the Shuttle and International Space Station and is highly conservative. Paper NASA is adventurous and promotes long-range venture but never secures adequate funding for its visions.[116] The coming months will determine whether George W Bush's speech of 14 January 2004 repeats this familiar pattern of hype followed by disappointment.

Refuelling our rocket dreams

The pressing task for the space community within industry, academia and government is to develop new symbols and a new language with which to project an image of space that can connect with wider society. The remainder of this chapter suggests three areas where space has the potential to play an ongoing role in shaping our social imagination.

Connexity

As described in Chapter 2, one of the most significant contributions that space has made is in triggering a new environmental consciousness. This is one part of what Geoff Mulgan has described as a deepening sense of global connexity.[117] Just as Earth's environment is a connected whole, social systems are increasingly linked, through culture, markets, media and finance. Space technology not only provides us with an awareness of global connectedness; it also gives us the tools to create an ever richer web of communications. The new space age will be all about empowering a diversity of connections and enabling relationships that were not previously possible. Without satellite technology, Manuel Castells' 'network society' would not exist.[118]

The challenge now is to extend and deepen the network society. At the moment, communication networks are characterised by inequality between the network rich and the network poor. Space technologies can help to build connexity, extending the reach of networks into places that other technologies cannot reach. By harnessing the power of satellites, developing countries can leapfrog conventional land-based networks, so helping to bridge the digital divide.

Public space

Over the past five years public space has risen up the agenda of urban and community renewal. The definition of a public space, according to urban theorists Reijndorp and Hajer, is one that is freely accessible to everyone. A good public space is one that is positively valued as a place of shared experiences by people from diverse backgrounds and interests.[119] It is also understood as a place for wonder and contemplation – 'bound up with ideas of expanding one's mental horizons of experiment, adventure, discovery and surprise'.[120]

Public space is integral to our basic conceptions of government and society: a shared public realm that sets the framework for our private endeavours and discoveries, but is maintained by our collective institutions and choices. Understanding public space in this way – as a domain of exploration and human agency – offers a helpful way to think afresh about outer space. It allows us to place the everyday life of a neighbourhood or town within the same frame of reference as the exploration of distant planets.

One of the most important roles that outer space performs is as an arena for imagining alternative futures. The Hilton's Lunar Hotel is a good expression of this. Numerous others can be found in film and fiction. As far back as 1902, *La Voyage dans la Lune* – arguably the first ever film with a plot – was about a journey to outer space. And perhaps the most famous and enduring example of this desire to imagine alternative futures in space is *Star Trek*.

Another reason public space is valued is as the place where we encounter 'the other' – strangers or outsiders, people outside our usual circle of family, friends and work. Similarly, outer space is the place where we can encounter the ultimate 'other' – extra-terrestrial life.

For space to work as public space, openness and accessibility are key. Currently, the UK space community fails this test. It is dominated by two groups – industry experts and amateur enthusiasts – whose average profile is white, male and middle-aged. Children are also excited by space, as shown by the popularity of the space exhibits at the Science Museum and the National Space Centre at Leicester, but this enthusiasm is rarely converted into longer-term engagement with space.

So how can the space community increase levels of openness and participation? Sir Martin Rees, the Astronomer Royal, predicts that over the next decade advances in computing will enable access to astronomy data that in the past was only available to a minority:

Detailed maps of the sky will be available to anyone who can access them or download them from the internet. There will be virtual observatories. Enthusiasts anywhere in the world will be able to participate in exploring our cosmic habitat, checking their own hunches, seeking out new patterns and discovering unusual objects.[121]

Construction has already begun on the UK-led Astro-Grid e-science network, which will merge colossal data sets from astronomy. The first stage is due to be complete in 2004 and could be a first step towards Sir Martin's vision of a public library of space data.

Efforts to increase access are also being made by the art world. Participation was a theme of Alessandra Mir's performance art piece *First Woman on the Moon*, which was recently shown at the Institute of Contemporary Arts in London. Staged among lunar craters carved out of a Dutch beach by JCBs, Mir's creation invited fellow beach goers to play in the lunar landscape. The American artist Craig Kalpakjian is planning, with the aid of a robot rover, to make a piece of art for the Moon. On the phone to Demos from his studio in New York, he explained the rationale: 'It's the first work of art that is really for the entire human race. Everyone could see it…Bringing art and aesthetics into space extends things a little, adding a certain complexity to our idea of space and what it can do for us.'[122]

The quest for ultimate meaning

One of the most valuable aspects of space is that it encourages, even obliges, us to engage with the really big questions that confront us, such as 'Why are we here?' and 'What is our place in the Universe?' Within the day-to-day routines of our lives, or the short electoral cycles of politics, such questions are rarely aired.

Given the likely advances in space science over the next decade, it is possible that some of these questions will move centre-stage. If astrobiologists succeed in their search for life beyond Earth, space science could become the locus for a deeper public conversation about the purpose and destination of human activity, and the need for new forms of global – or even interplanetary! – governance.

The impact of a greater understanding of what Sir Martin Rees calls 'our cosmic habitat' would be profound. Carl Sagan uses the term 'the Great Demotions' to describe the successive shifts in human perceptions of our place in the Universe that have occurred since Copernicus. 'Once we overcome our fear of being tiny, we find ourselves on the threshold of a vast and awesome Universe.'[123] Just how awesome that Universe might be is indicated by one rather mind-expanding equation. In the early 1960s astronomer Frank Drake devised a formula for estimating the number of advance civilisations that may exist in our galaxy:

$$R^{\star} \times f_e \times n_e \times f_1 \times f_i \times f_p \times L = N^{\star}$$ [124]

This calculation is based on the number of star formations over the lifetime of the Universe, the fraction of stars with planetary systems, and then estimates of the fraction of those that have suitable environments, intelligent life and technological civilisation. Setting very low estimates on each of the variables, Drake's grand total (N) for the number of extant technologically advanced civilisations in our galaxy is a whopping 1 million.

Scientists are currently divided into two camps on the question of whether we are alone in the Universe. On one side are the 'rare Earthers', who view Earth as a unique accident of chemistry; on the other side there are those who believe that the Universe is driven by a 'cosmic imperative' that is biased in favour of life. As Paul Davies observes,

The search for life elsewhere in the Universe is therefore the testing ground for two diametrically opposed world views. On the one hand is orthodox science, with its nihilistic philosophy of the pointlessness of the Universe, of impersonal laws oblivious of ends, a cosmos in which life and mind, science and art, hope and fear are but fluky incidental embellishments on a tapestry of irreversible cosmic corruption. On the other hand, there is an alternative view, undeniably romantic...it is a vision of a self-organising and self-complexifying universe, governed by ingenious laws that encourage matter to evolve towards life and consciousness. A universe where the emergence of thinking beings is a fundamental and integral part of the overall schemes of things. A universe in which we are not alone.[125]

Even though we have known since the sixteenth century that we are not the centre of the Universe, we continue to act in our everyday lives and thinking as if we are, and even forget that we are a part of a wider universe. We continually forget that space is not somewhere out there. We are already in space, spinning round the Sun aboard what is effectively Spaceship Earth. Equally forgotten is the fact that we are essentially made of stardust, our every atom continually recycled since the Universe exploded into existence with the big bang. Perhaps, as Frank White argues, it is time for us to begin to think of ourselves as 'terranauts' – citizen astronauts of the Earth.[126]

Let there be starlight

One practical way of reconnecting us to our cosmic habitat would be to tackle the light pollution that now obscures the night sky above Britain. Research published in 2003 by the Campaign for the Protection of Rural England (CPRE) shows that the amount of light shining upwards across England rose by 24 per cent over seven years. The south-east of England now has only 1 per cent of its dark skies left, and some regions are entirely light-saturated at night. As a result, entire generations of children are growing up having never seen the Milky Way, and serious astronomers are being forced to travel abroad in pursuit of dark skies.[127]

Street lighting and commercial developments such as petrol stations, freight depots and sports facilities are largely to blame for this trend. CPRE has called for tougher planning controls aimed at curbing light pollution, a recommendation that has since been echoed by the House of Commons select committee on science and technology. There are several practical measures that can reduce the problem: for example, lights could be redirected downwards or fitted with shields; and developers could be forced to make light pollution assessments. If such pollution is ignored, it will impoverish our experience of space and limit its inspirational power.

6. Black sky thinking: a manifesto for public space

For the first time since the end of the Cold War, there is a growing recognition that space matters. George W Bush has made it a central focus of his second-term electoral platform. The European Union has produced its first fully fledged space strategy. China, India and others are investing millions to join the ranks of the leading space nations.

But there is no consensus yet about *how* space will matter. Competing stories are being told about the real value and future significance of space, ranging from the zealous optimism of Bush's frontier vision to the cautious pragmatism of the UK government's approach.

This report argues that the time is ripe for Britain to develop a new vision of *public space*. This vision has five core dimensions:

○ It is *distinctively European*, grounded in a commitment to international development and environmental protection.
○ It sees space as a crucial part of the *smart state*, contributing to economic innovation and public service renewal.
○ It recognises the *intrinsic value of space science and earth observation* in understanding the origins of the Universe and our place within it.
○ It reconnects space with our *social and cultural imagination*.

○ It *democratises space* by developing new forms of public
participation that can shape the future direction of space
science and technology.

There are many routes through which progress towards this vision
could be achieved. In this final chapter we suggest six initial steps that
government and others could take.

1. *Renew our national commitment to space*
    After the honourable failure of Beagle 2, the UK needs to
    signal that it will play a leadership role in developing
    innovative space missions at the leading edge of science.
    For example, for less than the price of one Beagle a year,
    the UK could place itself at the heart of the Aurora
    programme. UK participation in the first, robotic phase of
    Aurora would require around £25 million of extra
    investment each year for five years.
2. *Undertake a strategic audit of Britain in space*
    New money is only part of the equation. There is a greater
    need for those within and beyond the space community
    to embrace a shift in perspective. Policy-makers, in
    particular, should pay closer attention to the strategic
    significance of space and the contribution it can make to
    wider economic, social and environmental goals. To
    encourage fresh perspectives on space, the government –
    perhaps led by the Cabinet Office – should undertake a
    strategic audit of the wider potential of space science and
    technologies, in order to determine where the UK should
    focus its future investment.
3. *Extend involvement in space across government*
    A broader range of government departments should
    contribute to space policy and the identification of new
    space applications. Key departments to involve include
    transport, environment and international development.
    Space is already making a real contribution to policy and

delivery in each of these areas, but more could be achieved through deeper and more sustained efforts at joint working.

4. *Support open innovation*
    As a network organisation, the British National Space Centre is ideally placed to promote open, networked models of innovation across industrial and space science. This approach should be made explicit in BNSC's mission statement and operating structures, and it should actively draw on learning from elsewhere such as the open source movement. As Lord Sainsbury has noted: 'BNSC is the means by which we work together. BNSC brings together in one partnership organisation all of our interests in civil space.'[128]

5. *Embrace diversity*
    Some 30 per cent of those working in space are due to retire by 2015, and the average age of space scientists and industrialists is increasing by a year every year.[129] The space community is facing a crisis of creativity, and there is a pressing need to attract a younger, more diverse range of people into space science and industry. The wave of interest generated by Beagle 2 shows what can be achieved with a little imagination. Lessons should be drawn from this and applied elsewhere.

6. *Build new coalitions for space*
    The space community should build new links across local government, NGOs and community groups. Touchstone issues such as combating light pollution could be used to reconnect with a broader set of stakeholders in a new way. There is particular scope for new alliances between the environmental movement and space scientists, born out of a recognition of the contribution that earth observation can make to sustainable development.

References

1   US President George W Bush, speech, 14 Jan 2004.
2   A James, *New Statesman*, 15 Dec 2003.
3   F Spufford, *Backroom Boys* (London: Faber, 2003).
4   P Murdin, 'Mars or bust for farmer's space mission', *Observer*, 30 Nov 2003.
5   See Figure 1 in Chapter 1, page 39
6   M Rees, 'Our greatest quest', *New Scientist*, 12 July 2003.
7   JF Kennedy, speech to Rice University, 12 Sept 1962.
8   M Benjamin, 'Sentimental journey', *Guardian*, 16 Dec 2002.
9   Space Frontier Association, *Manifesto for the Frontier:testimony to the Space and Aeronautics Subcommittee of the US House of Representatives*, 16 March 1995.
10 B Chase, Demos interview, 24 June 2003.
11 BNSC, *UK Draft Space Strategy 2003–2006* (British National Space Centre, 2003).
12 Lord Sainsbury, speech to the first meeting of the Space Strategy Council, 4 Dec 2002.
13 M O'Neill, 'Parliament and the stars', *New Statesman* supplement.
14 Unattributed interview with Demos, June 2003.
15 BNSC, *UK Draft Space Strategy 2003–2006*.
16 The Project for the New American Century, *Rebuilding America's Defences: strategy, forces and resources for a new century* (Washington DC: PNAC, 2000).
17 Ibid.
18 Executive Summary; in *Report of the Commission to Assess United States National Security Space Management and Organisation* (Washington DC, 11 Jan, 2001).
19 The US defence expenditure of $399.1 billion in 2004 is more than ten times the UK's expenditure of $38.4 billion.
20 ESA, *The European Space Sector in a Global Context: ESA's annual analysis 2002* (Paris: European Space Agency, 2002).
21 M Krepon and C Clary, *Space Assurance or Space Dominance? The case against weaponizing space* (Washington DC: The Henry L Stimson Center, 2003).

22   R Johnson, *Space without Weapons: ballistic missile defence and the weaponisation of space* (Washington DC: The Acronym Institute, 2003), *www.acronym.org*.

23   Ibid.

24   Treaty on Principles Governing the Activities of States in the Exploration and Use of Outer Space, 1967.

25   UN resolution A/RES/55/32. Prevention of an arms race in outer space, 20 Nov 2000

26   Michael R. Gordon, 'US tries defusing Allies' Opposition to Missile Defense', *New York Times*, 4 Feb 2001.

27   Full text available at: www.europaworld.org/week101/weaponrace181002.htm.

28   EC, *European Space Policy*, green paper EUR 20459 (Brussels: European Commission, 2003).

29   J-J Dordain, Demos interview, 13 June 2003.

30   R Kagan, *Paradise and Power: America and Europe in the new world order* (London: Atlantic Books, 2003).

31   Ibid.

32   EC, *European Space Policy*.

33   Ibid.

34   *International Herald Tribune*, 19 Dec 2001.

35   *Financial Times*, 18 Sept 2003.

36   R Oosterlick, Demos interview, 13 June 2003.

37   Radio–Television News Directors' Assocation and Foundation, press release, 7 Nov 2001.

38   Kagan, *Paradise and Power*.

39   Krepon and Clary, *Space Assurance or Space Dominance?*

40   R Johnson, *Space without Weapons*.

41   Krepon and Clary, *Space Assurance or Space Dominance?*.

42   Ibid.

43   European Convention, *Draft Treaty establishing a Constitution for Europe*, 10 July 2003, http://europa.eu.int/futurum/constitution/table/index_en.htm.

44   I Christie, *Breaking with Convention: towards a new European future* (London: Green Alliance, 2003).

45   N Butler, 'Future Perfect Union', *Foreign Policy*, Jan–Feb 2003.

46   Kagan, *Paradise and Power*.

47   H Chesbrough, *Open Innovation: the new imperative for creating and profiting from technology* (Boston, Mass: Harvard Business School Press, 2003).

48   Available at: www.esa.int/export/esaCP/GGGZM2D3KCC_index_2.html.

49   See http://unosat.web.cern.ch.

50   Available at: http://europa.eu.int/comm/space/articles/news/news54_en.html.

51   EC, *European Space Policy*.

52   R Johnson, *Space without Weapons*.

53   R Brook, Demos interview, 19 September 2003.

54   Sir M Sweeting, Demos interview, 7 May 2003.

55   C Cookson, 'First satellite constellation will open window on world's natural disasters' *Financial Times*, 8 Sept 2003.

56   BNSC, *UK Draft Space Strategy 2003–2006.*

57   T Bentley and J Wilsdon (eds), *The Adaptive State: strategies for personalising the public realm* (London: Demos, 2003).

58   Commission for Integrated Transport, *Paying for Road Use* (London: CfIT, Feb 2002).

59   J Foley and M Ferguson, *Putting the Brakes on Climate Change* (London: IPPR, 2003).

60   Silicon.com, 'Orange is on the buses to reduce delays', 20 Oct 2003.

61   J Wilsdon and D Stedman Jones, *The Politics of Bandwidth: network innovation and regulation in Broadband Britain* (London: Demos, 2002).

62   EC, *European Space Policy.*

63   *Financial Times*, 27 Oct 2003.

64   'Across the great divide', *Guardian*, 10 Dec 2003.

65   See for example N Curthoys and J Crabtree, *SmartGov: renewing electronic government for improved service delivery* (London: Work Foundation, 2003); Wilsdon and Stedman Jones *Politics of Bandwidth*; Ian Kearns, *Code Red* (London: IPPR, 2002).

66   D Barvor, presentation to ESA symposium Telemedicine via Satellite in the Information Society, 23–24 May 2003.

67   J Gill, Demos interview, 25 Apr 2003.

68   Edward Luce, 'A space programme for the people', *Financial Times*, 10 March 2003.

69   Ibid.

70   James Meek, 'Satellite to check on Earth's health', *Guardian*, 21 February 2002

71   S Jasanoff, 'Image and Imagination: the formation of global environmental consciousness', in *Changing the Atmosphere*, eds C Miller and P Edwards (Cambridge, MA: MIT Press, 2001).

72   S Wilson, Demos interview, May 2003.

73   R Gurney, Demos interview, 1 May 2003.

74   J Achache, speech at Demos seminar, 3 June 2003.

75   R Sharpe, Demos interview, 19 June 2003.

76   Euroconsult, 2002.

77   EC, *European Space Policy.*

78   BNSC–ESYS, *Size and Health of the UK Space Industry: 2001 update study* (London: BNSC, 2001).

79   OECD International Futures Programme, *The Commercialisation of Space: long term prospects and implications: report on the consultation process* (Paris: Organisation for Economic Co-operation and Development, June 2002).

80   Futron–Office of Space Commercialization, *Trends in Space Commerce* (Washington DC: Department of Commerce, 2001); DFI International *Market Opportunities in Space: the near-term roadmap* (Washington DC: Department of Commerce, Dec 2002).

81   D Southwood, unpublished comments on the *UK Draft Space Strategy.*

82   D Ashford, *Spaceflight Revolution* (London: World Scientific Publishing, 2003).

83   DFI International, *Market Opportunities in Space*.

84   Futron–Office of Space Commercialization, *Trends in Space Commerce*.

85   Ibid.

86   M Porter, *UK Competitiveness: moving to the next stage* (London: DTI–ESRC, 2003).

87   C Freeman and F Louca, *As Time Goes By: from the industrial revolutions to the information revolution* (Oxford: OUP, 2001).

88   CM Christensen, *The Innovator's Dilemma* (Harvard Business School Press, 1997).

89   DFI International, *Market Opportunities in Space*.

90   R Armstrong, Demos interview, 6 May 2003.

91   World Tourism Organisation.

92   Sir M Sweeting, Demos interview, 7 May 2003.

93   *General Public Space Travel and Tourism* (NASA and Space Transport Association, 1997).

94   Future Space Transportation Study, 'Andrews Space and Technology under NASA', NRA 8-27, 2001. Cited in DFI International, *Market Opportunities in Space*.

95   DFI International, *Market Opportunities in Space*.

96   Cited in R Armstrong, *Space Architecture* (London: Wiley, 2000).

97   Available at: www.bizreport.com/article.php?art_id=5855.

98   Available at: www.lunarcorp.com.

99   J Taylor, Demos interview, 28 April 2003.

100 Available at: www.lunarcorp.com.

101 Ibid.

102 Dr K Fong, Demos interview, 8 April 2003.

103 L Bergreen, *The Quest for Mars: the NASA scientists and their search for life beyond earth* (London: Harper Collins, 2001).

104 P Davies, *The Origin of Life* (London: Penguin, 1999).

105 G Gilmore, Demos interview, 5 June 2003.

106 Written comments to Demos.

107 A Keiper, 'A new vision for NASA', *New Atlantis*, no 3, fall 2003.

108 See for example the House of Lords report *Science and Society* (2000).

109 ESA, *Aurora Programme – Executive Summary* (Paris: European Space Agency, 27 Nov 2003).

110 Lucian of Samosata, *Icaromenippus, an Aerial Expedition* (c.120–180 AD).

111 HE McCurdy, *Space and the American Imagination* (Washington DC: Smithsonian Books 1999).

112 R Zubrin, telephone interview, 3 June 2003.

113 S Topham, *Where's May Space Age: the rise and fall of futuristic design* (London: Prestal, 2003).

114 Ibid.

115 McCurdy, *Space and the American Imagination*.

116 M Benjamin, *Rocket Dreams: How the Space Age Shaped Our Vision of a World Beyond* (London: Vintage, 2003)

117 G Mulgan, *Connexity: responsibility, freedom, business and power in the new century* (Vintage, London 1998)

118 M Castells, *The Rise of the Network Society* (London: Blackwell, 2000)

119 A Reijndorp and M Hajer, *In Search of the New Public Domain* (Netherlands Architecture Institute, Amsterdam 2001).

120 F Bianchini and H Schwengel, 'Re-imagining the city', *Enterprise and Heritage: Crosscurrents of national culture*, eds J Corner and S Harvey (London: Routledge, 1991).

121 M Rees, *Our Cosmic Habitat* (London: Orion, 2001).

122 C Kalpakjian, telephone interview, 11 June 2003.

123 Cited in McCurdy, *Space and the American Imagination*.

124 R^* is the average rate of star formation over the lifetime of the galaxy
f_e the fraction of stars with planetary systems
n_e the number of planets per star with ecological suitable environments
f_l the fraction of planets (ne) on which life arises
f_i the fraction of planets (f1) on which intelligence develops
f_p the fraction of planets (f1) on which technological civilisations arise
L the lifetime of the high-tech civilisations
N^* the number of extant technological civilisations in the galaxy.

125 P Davies, *The Origin of Life*.

126 F White, *The Overview Effect: space exploration and human evolution* (Reston VA: AIAA, 1998).

127 J Vidal, 'Floodlit Britain blots out stars', *Guardian*, 10 May 2003.

128 Lord Sainsbury, speech to Space Strategy Council, 4 Dec 2002.

129 BNSC, *UK Draft Space Strategy 2003-2006* (London: HMSO, 2003)

DEMOS – Licence to Publish

1. **Definitions**
   a **"Collective Work"** means a work, such as a periodical issue, anthology or encyclopedia, in which the Work in its entirety in unmodified form, along with a number of other contributions, constituting separate and independent works in themselves, are assembled into a collective whole. A work that constitutes a Collective Work will not be considered a Derivative Work (as defined below) for the purposes of this Licence.
   b **"Derivative Work"** means a work based upon the Work or upon the Work and other pre-existing works, such as a musical arrangement, dramatization, fictionalization, motion picture version, sound recording, art reproduction, abridgment, condensation, or any other form in which the Work may be recast, transformed, or adapted, except that a work that constitutes a Collective Work or a translation from English into another language will not be considered a Derivative Work for the purpose of this Licence.
   c **"Licensor"** means the individual or entity that offers the Work under the terms of this Licence.
   d **"Original Author"** means the individual or entity who created the Work.
   e **"Work"** means the copyrightable work of authorship offered under the terms of this Licence.
   f **"You"** means an individual or entity exercising rights under this Licence who has not previously violated the terms of this Licence with respect to the Work, or who has received express permission from DEMOS to exercise rights under this Licence despite a previous violation.
2. **Fair Use Rights.** Nothing in this licence is intended to reduce, limit, or restrict any rights arising from fair use, first sale or other limitations on the exclusive rights of the copyright owner under copyright law or other applicable laws.
3. **Licence Grant.** Subject to the terms and conditions of this Licence, Licensor hereby grants You a worldwide, royalty-free, non-exclusive, perpetual (for the duration of the applicable copyright) licence to exercise the rights in the Work as stated below:
   a to reproduce the Work, to incorporate the Work into one or more Collective Works, and to reproduce the Work as incorporated in the Collective Works;
   b to distribute copies or phonorecords of, display publicly, perform publicly, and perform publicly by means of a digital audio transmission the Work including as incorporated in Collective Works;
   The above rights may be exercised in all media and formats whether now known or hereafter devised. The above rights include the right to make such modifications as are technically necessary to exercise the rights in other media and formats. All rights not expressly granted by Licensor are hereby reserved.
4. **Restrictions.** The licence granted in Section 3 above is expressly made subject to and limited by the following restrictions:
   a You may distribute, publicly display, publicly perform, or publicly digitally perform the Work only under the terms of this Licence, and You must include a copy of, or the Uniform Resource Identifier, for this Licence with every copy or phonorecord of the Work You distribute, publicly display, publicly perform, or publicly digitally perform. You may not offer or impose any terms on the Work that alter or restrict the terms of this Licence or the recipients' exercise of the rights granted hereunder. You may not sublicence the Work. You must keep intact all notices that refer to this Licence and to the disclaimer of warranties. You may not distribute, publicly display, publicly perform, or publicly digitally perform the Work with any technological measures that control access or use of the Work in a manner inconsistent with the terms of this Licence Agreement. The above applies to the Work as incorporated in a Collective Work, but this does not require the Collective Work apart from the Work itself to be made subject to the terms of this Licence. If You create a Collective Work, upon notice from any Licencor You must, to the extent practicable, remove from the Collective Work any reference to such Licensor or the Original Author, as requested.
   b You may not exercise any of the rights granted to You in Section 3 above in any manner that is primarily intended for or directed toward commercial advantage or private monetary

compensation. The exchange of the Work for other copyrighted works by means of digital file-sharing or otherwise shall not be considered to be intended for or directed toward commercial advantage or private monetary compensation, provided there is no payment of any monetary compensation in connection with the exchange of copyrighted works.

c If you distribute, publicly display, publicly perform, or publicly digitally perform the Work or any Collective Works, You must keep intact all copyright notices for the Work and give the Original Author credit reasonable to the medium or means You are utilizing by conveying the name (or pseudonym if applicable) of the Original Author if supplied; the title of the Work if supplied. Such credit may be implemented in any reasonable manner; provided, however, that in the case of a Collective Work, at a minimum such credit will appear where any other comparable authorship credit appears and in a manner at least as prominent as such other comparable authorship credit.

5. **Representations, Warranties and Disclaimer**

a By offering the Work for public release under this Licence, Licensor represents and warrants that, to the best of Licensor's knowledge after reasonable inquiry:

i Licensor has secured all rights in the Work necessary to grant the licence rights hereunder and to permit the lawful exercise of the rights granted hereunder without You having any obligation to pay any royalties, compulsory licence fees, residuals or any other payments;

ii The Work does not infringe the copyright, trademark, publicity rights, common law rights or any other right of any third party or constitute defamation, invasion of privacy or other tortious injury to any third party.

b EXCEPT AS EXPRESSLY STATED IN THIS LICENCE OR OTHERWISE AGREED IN WRITING OR REQUIRED BY APPLICABLE LAW, THE WORK IS LICENCED ON AN "AS IS" BASIS, WITHOUT WARRANTIES OF ANY KIND, EITHER EXPRESS OR IMPLIED INCLUDING, WITHOUT LIMITATION, ANY WARRANTIES REGARDING THE CONTENTS OR ACCURACY OF THE WORK.

6. **Limitation on Liability.** EXCEPT TO THE EXTENT REQUIRED BY APPLICABLE LAW, AND EXCEPT FOR DAMAGES ARISING FROM LIABILITY TO A THIRD PARTY RESULTING FROM BREACH OF THE WARRANTIES IN SECTION 5, IN NO EVENT WILL LICENSOR BE LIABLE TO YOU ON ANY LEGAL THEORY FOR ANY SPECIAL, INCIDENTAL, CONSEQUENTIAL, PUNITIVE OR EXEMPLARY DAMAGES ARISING OUT OF THIS LICENCE OR THE USE OF THE WORK, EVEN IF LICENSOR HAS BEEN ADVISED OF THE POSSIBILITY OF SUCH DAMAGES.

7. **Termination**

a This Licence and the rights granted hereunder will terminate automatically upon any breach by You of the terms of this Licence. Individuals or entities who have received Collective Works from You under this Licence, however, will not have their licences terminated provided such individuals or entities remain in full compliance with those licences. Sections 1, 2, 5, 6, 7, and 8 will survive any termination of this Licence.

b Subject to the above terms and conditions, the licence granted here is perpetual (for the duration of the applicable copyright in the Work). Notwithstanding the above, Licensor reserves the right to release the Work under different licence terms or to stop distributing the Work at any time; provided, however that any such election will not serve to withdraw this Licence (or any other licence that has been, or is required to be, granted under the terms of this Licence), and this Licence will continue in full force and effect unless terminated as stated above.

8. Miscellaneous

a Each time You distribute or publicly digitally perform the Work or a Collective Work, DFMOS offers to the recipient a licence to the Work on the same terms and conditions as the licence granted to You under this Licence.

b If any provision of this Licence is invalid or unenforceable under applicable law, it shall not affect the validity or enforceability of the remainder of the terms of this Licence, and without further action by the parties to this agreement, such provision shall be reformed to the minimum extent necessary to make such provision valid and enforceable.

c No term or provision of this Licence shall be deemed waived and no breach consented to unless such waiver or consent shall be in writing and signed by the party to be charged with such waiver or consent.

d This Licence constitutes the entire agreement between the parties with respect to the Work licensed here. There are no understandings, agreements or representations with respect to the Work not specified here. Licensor shall not be bound by any additional provisions that may appear in any communication from You. This Licence may not be modified without the mutual written agreement of DEMOS and You.